English Up Book 1

Kyungbok University Language Education Center

Series Editors: *Bo Taig Kwon, Curtis MacDonald*

Series Authors: *Alun Cave, Kristina Chang, Declan Griffin, Bo Taig Kwon, Bridget Leathwick, Curtis MacDonald, Julien Poncet, Claudio Stickar, Don Urban*

도서출판 | 동인

Published by Dongin Publishing Co
118, 5, Hyehwa-ro 3-gil, Jongno-gu, Seoul, Korea (03075)
Tel: (02) 765-7145, Fax: (02) 765-7165, Email: dongin60@chollian.net, Homepage: donginbook.co.kr

ISBN 978-89-5506-695-1 13740

정가: *20,000* 원

Table of Contents

WELCOME TO ENGLISH UP BOOK 1

MEET THE AUTHORS:

Alun Cave

Alun Cave has been an EFL teacher in Korea since 2003. In addition to providing language education to thousands of students, he also promotes continuous professional development, and has organized workshops on the use of technology in the classroom. As one of the founding members of the English program at Kyungbok University, Alun Cave has helped bring KBU's Language Education Center to the forefront of English instruction in Korea. He also has a great sense of humour.

Kristina Chang

Kristina Chang is currently a professor at Kyungbok University. Before coming to Korea, she worked as a research scientist in the University of Washington School of Medicine for four years. Subsequently, she has a background in scientific writing and has been published twice in the Journal of Virology. She is fluent in both English and Korean and contributes her bilingual background to her ability to understand and teach the fundamental patterns found in language.

Declan Griffin

Declan Griffin is one of the newer recruits at Kyungbok University. He has a vast amount of experience teaching English as a foreign language to different levels and groups in Korea. Declan has been teaching in Korea for 8 years and this has been central to his development as a teacher. Declan is delighted to have contributed to the book and hopes the students embrace it and feel proud of doing so.

Bo Taig Kwon

Bo Taig Kwon taught English and English literature in Sogang University for 5 years and has been in Kyungbok University since 2001. Based upon his experiences in Newcastle University, England and in Sogang University, he tries to focus on communicative language teaching, let alone basic matters such as vocabulary and an intermediate level of grammar.

Bridget Leathwick

Bridget Leathwick has been teaching English in South Korea for the past 8 years. She has taught a wide variety of ages and levels during her time in Korea. This has given her a solid knowledge foundation for her contribution to the book development at Kyungbok University. In her native New Zealand, Bridget is a Registered Nurse. She loves working with people in a supportive and educational role, which both nursing and teaching require.

Curtis MacDonald

Curtis MacDonald has been an English instructor for over a decade, all within Korea. His experiences in and out of the classroom inspire his section of the book. He believes any student can be successful in English. It is his hope that students can restart their studies in a fun and meaningful way in this book.

Julien Poncet

Julien Poncet started teaching English as a second language in Boston, USA, almost 10 years ago. His students came from all around the world, especially South Korea. It is based on their recommendation that he decided to pursue his teaching adventure in Korea, which he now calls home.

Claudio Stickar

Claudio Stickar has been a Master Printer for over 25 years having worked with blue chip contemporary artists creating graphic editions that have been shown at major museums and collections around the world. Mr. Stickar has presented talks, given lectures and demonstrations on his craft for art organizations and educational institutions in both the US and Korea. He still maintains his own studio creating editions with mid-career and emerging artists.

Don Urban

Don Urban hails from Cobalt, Ontario and is a graduate of Bishop's University. He has taught at every level in the Korean education system. His passion for technology and internet learning has enhanced the lives of countless students. Professor Urban also has a strong background in history and sociology and uses those skills to bring a deep cultural awareness to any classroom. A strong believer that a teacher is always a student, he constantly challenges himself to learn and develop his profession.

WELCOME UNIT:

Welcome to the English Up Series. This series was created to give everyone, from false beginner to high intermediate, a chance to be successful in English. It has several interesting features.

A. **Warm-up Questions:** This section is to prepare the student for talking using common questions and helping the student to speak in full sentences. The secondary goal is to prepare the students for a job interview, whether it be in response to common questions or in self introduction form.

기본 질문: 이 부분은 학생들로 하여금 일상적인 질문을 활용하여 대화할 수 있도록 준비시키고 온전한 문장으로 말할 수 있게 도와주는 부분입니다. 두 번째 목적은 입사면접에서 활용할 수 있는 일상적 질문에 관한 답변 또는 자기소개를 할 수 있게 준비시키는 것입니다.

B. **Dialogues:** The dialogue section is to give the student exposure to real conversation and, combined with the substitution exercise, to allow the student to prepare and practice the conversations. The substitution exercise will allow for flexibility in conversation and an increase in vocabulary. In many cases, the replaced dialogue piece is a common slang or colloquial, which are often hard to understand to the second language learner.

대화: 대화 부분은 학생들로 하여금 실생활에 활용되는 회화를 접할 수 있게 해 주고 대입식의 방법을 활용하여 학생들이 회화를 준비하고 연습할 수 있도록 해 줍니다. 대입연습을 통해 대화시 융통성을 발휘할 수 있고 어휘력을 증진시킬 수 있습니다. 대체하여 사용하는 회화표현은 일상적인 속어 또는 구어체 표현인데 외국어로 영어를 배우는 학생들이 이해하기에 종종 어려운 경우가 많습니다.

C. **Conversation Corner:** This section helps to prepare the student for real world conversation, both in the workplace and on the street. The secondary goal is to teach the students how to be respectful and use honorifics in English.

대화 부분: 이 부분은 직장이나 거리에서 발생할 수 있는 실제 상황에 대처할 수 있는 능력을 향상시킵니다. 두 번째 목적은 영어에서 경칭과 존대말을 사용하는 방법을 가르치는 것입니다.

D. **Grammar Gallery:** The grammar starts at the basic level and builds up to cover most of the major tenses in English. Beyond using a pattern and repeating it, the grammar gallary compares and contrasts grammar in regard to usage and helps the student to recognize not only how to use the grammar, but when to use the grammar. This section will also reflect the grammar questions used in the TOEIC test whenever possible.

문법 부분: 기본 사항을 위시하여 영어의 대부분의 시제를 다루게 됩니다. 문형 반복 훈련을 뛰어넘어 용법과 관련한 비교와 대조를 하면서 학생들이 문법을 언제 어떻게 활용해야 하는지를 느끼게 지도합니다. 이 부분은 또한 가능할 때마다 토익에서 활용되는 문법 문제를 반영합니다.

E. **TOEIC Vocabulary:** One of the biggest factors in mastering a language and a test is the building of vocabulary. This book expects the student to take responsibilty for their own education. We will introduce almost 1,000 new words in this series, words that are frequently used in conversation and in TOEIC. Often these words will be assigned as homework, or self study. It is the student responsibilty to make themselves proficient in the provided vocabulary.

토익 빈출어휘: 외국어 학습과 외국어 시험에서 가장 큰 요소 중 하나는 어휘력 향상입니다. 본 교재는 학생들이 자신의 학습을 스스로 하기를 기대합니다. 회화에 자주 사용되며 토익에도 출제되는 대략 1,000개의 어휘를 이 부분에서 취급합니다. 이 어휘들은 과제용 또는 자습용입니다. 주어진 어휘를 활용하는 것은 학생들의 몫입니다.

F. **Other:** As the level progresses, different sections such as TOEIC preparation/phrasal verbs and idioms/and career concentration will be added. These will help the student in the growing pyramid of knowledge and help them to understand and use English better.
기타: 단계를 밟아갈수록 토익 준비와 동사구, 숙어 그리고 직업관련 내용과 같은 새로운 내용이 추가됩니다. 이런 내용은 점점 쌓여만 가는 거대한 지식의 피라미드 속에서 학생들에게 도움을 줄 것이고 영어를 보다 더 잘 이해하고 활용하는 데 도움을 줄 것입니다.

CLASSROOM ETIQUETTE

1. Students are expected to be at their desk with all the appropriate materials (book, pencil, pen, notebook, etc.) at the beginning of class. Being late is disrespectful to the professor and to the students who are ready for class to begin on time.
수업이 시작되면 학생들은 필요한 준비물(교재, 필기구 공책 등)을 지참하고 책상에 앉아있어야 합니다. 지각은 정시에 수업을 시작할 준비가 되어있는 학생 및 교수님에게 실례를 범하는 것입니다.

2. Cell phones can be used in class to help the student understand. There are dictionary translations and certain apps that can expand the student's breadth of knowledge. However, too many students use their phone to text message or surf the internet. Cell phones should be put away out of sight in a bag, not in the desk where it can be easily seen. All learning requires concentration and focus. Recent studies show that looking at the cell phone can disrupt the brain's attention and ability to learn for up to 17 minutes. So please understand that we ask you to put your cell phones away not as a punishment, but as a path to greater learning.
휴대전화는 학생들의 이해를 돕기 위해 활용될 수 있습니다. 학생들의 지식의 폭을 넓힐 수 있는 번역문과 앱이 있습니다. 그러나 너무 많은 학생들이 문자를 보내거나 인터넷 검색을 하기 위해 휴대전화를 사용합니다. 휴대전화는 책상 위에 두지 말고 가방에 보이지 않게 간직해야 합니다. 모든 학습에는 집중이 필요합니다. 최근의 연구에 의하면 휴대전화를 볼 경우 17분 동안 주의를 산만하게 한다고 합니다. 따라서 벌칙이 아니라 더 나은 학습을 위해 휴대전화를 보이지 않는 곳에 간직하라는 지시를 이해해 주기 바랍니다.

3. **Being an effective student:** The instructors can only do so much with the time they are given. It is the student's responsibility to be prepared to learn and practice the exercises. Each class, the instructor will give you opportunity to answer questions and practice dialogue with partners. Doing these exercises is crucial for improvement, as well as doing any homework assigned.
효과적인 학습을 하기 위해: 교수님들은 강의시간에 최선을 다합니다. 학생들은 배우고 연습할 준비가 되어있어야 합니다. 매 시간 교수님들은 학생들에게 대답할 기회를 줄 것이고 다른 학생들과 대화를 연습하도록 할 것입니다. 이런 연습은 주어진 과제를 수행하는 것만큼 영어실력 향상을 위해 중요한 것입니다.

4. **Have fun:** English does not have to be that daunting subject that causes stress and fear. It is a language and should be spoken and used to communicate. Be free to laugh and have fun if you make mistakes, as everyone will make mistakes, even native speakers. Enjoying a class can only reinforce the materials that we are trying to give you.
수업을 즐기세요: 영어는 스트레스와 공포를 자아내는 무서운 과목일 필요가 없습니다. 언어일 뿐이고 소통을 하기 위해 말하고 사용하는 것입니다. 누구나 실수하고 심지어 원어민들도 실수를 하니까 실수를 하더라도 자유롭게 웃고 즐기세요. 수업을 즐기면 교수님들이 학생들에게 제공하는 내용을 더 잘 이해할 수 있을 것입니다.

MEET THE CHARACTERS:

John Ellers

Gender: Male (boy)
Birthday: April 16, 1987
Age: 29
Phone number: Home: 070-6422-7021
Cell: 010-4380-9612
Address: 165 Eunsongcheong 2-ga, Susung-gu, Daegu, South Korea, 42402
Country of Birth: Portland, Oregon, U.S.A.
Family: Wife (Annie Richardson / Birthday: December 23, 1976 / 38 years old / homemaker)
Daughter (Penny Ellers / Birthday: April 13, 2012 / 2 years old / goes to a nursery)

ABOUT HIS LIFE:

Job now: English teacher in a hakwon (학원 / academy) / Student
Job before: Event security analyst

CAN:	CAN'T:
– play drums	– eat peanuts
– skip rope	– walk in the summer heat
– make his daughter laugh	– wear a necktie
	– smile at rude people

Chores: Look after daughter while wife takes a break, cook dinner 3 days a week, pick daughter up from pre-school, rub wife's feet
Wife: cook breakfast, wash dinner dishes, do laundry, care for child, vacuum, massage back of husband.
Yesterday: go shopping, cook dinner, go to nursing class, watch T.V., (Not: do homework, go clothes shopping, drink alcohol)
On vacation: listen to records, go skiing, watch movies, train for a marathon.
Spare time / free time: read a book, listen to music, play computer games, play with daughter

Jenny Belfort

Gender: Female (girl)
Birthday: January 27, 1992
Age: 24
Phone number: Home 031-7832-4532
Cell: 010-9645-3167
Address: 15 Hannam-dong, Yongsan-gu, Seoul, South Korea, 04410
Country of Birth: Edmonton, Alberta, Canada
Family: Boyfriend (Robert Kim / Birthday: June 3, 1990 / 24 years old / student)
0 children

ABOUT HER LIFE:

Job now: part timer in a bar / Student
Job before: Kindergarten teacher

CAN:
- sing
- speak sign language
- play volleyball

CAN'T:
- do math
- drink alcohol
- kick a soccer ball
- speak Korean

Chores: cook dinner, clean bathroom, vacuum, take out trash,
Roommate: cook breakfast, wash dinner dishes, do laundry
Yesterday: go shopping, cook dinner, go to nursing class, watch T.V.,
(Not: do homework, go clothes shopping, drink alcohol)
On vacation: meet family, camping with friends, watch movies, work at job.
Spare time / free time: read a book, listen to music, go to the singing room, go to the beach.

Akari Bando

Gender: Female (girl)
Birthday: August 2, 1988
Age: 28
Phone number: Home 031-4549-2851
Cell: 010-6668-0982
Address: 46 Songpa Street, Namyangju, Gyeonggi-do, South Korea, 12113
Country of Birth: Japan
Family: Husband (Akihiro Bando / Birthday: March 5 1976 / 32 years old / works as car engineer,)
1 daughter (Yui Bando / Birthday July 31, 2010 / 6 years old / goes to preschool)

ABOUT HER LIFE:

Job now: Homemaker / Student
Job before: Tax accountant

CAN:
- speak Japanese and some English
- work with numbers
- cook Italian food

CAN'T:
- sing
- dance
- play a musical instrument
- speak Korean

Chores: cook breakfast and dinner, do laundry, vacuum
Her husband: wash dinner dishes, take out trash, clean bathroom
Her daughter: pick up toys
Yesterday: cook dinner, go to English class, do laundry, watch T.V.,
(not play computer games, not go shopping, not drink coffee)
On vacation: usually go to the beach, swim, sit in the sun, make a sandcastle, relax, read a book
Spare time / free time: read a book, watch T.V., do a puzzle, do yoga, listen to music.

Ricardo Aguera

Gender: Male (boy)
Birthday: June 14, 1992
Age: 24
Phone number: Home 954 7825 4321
Cell: 654-998-723
Address: San Fernando 2, Old Town, Seville, Spain, 41004
Country of Birth: Spain
Family: younger brother
(Jesus Aguera / Birthday: August 10, 1995 / 21 years old / studies journalism at university)

ABOUT HIM:
Job now: part-time job as server at a hotel restaurant
Job before: dishwasher / food prep in a hotel kitchen

CAN:
- work at a busy restaurant
- play soccer
- cook paella

CAN'T:
- drive a car
- speak Korean
- play the piano

Chores: clean living room and bathroom, wash the dishes
Brother: mop floor, take out trash, do laundry, clean kitchen
Yesterday: play soccer, watch T.V. with brother, talk to girlfriend on phone
(Not cook breakfast, go shopping, watch a movie)
On vacation: go to the beach, do watersports, play soccer, go sightseeing
Spare time / free time: play games on cell phone, watch T.V., listen to music, think about future plans

Alex Ross

Gender: Male (boy)
Birthday: November 5, 1980
Age: 36
Phone number: Cell: 010-5261-0046
Address: 102-102, Xia Apt., Nonhyeon-dong, Gangnam-gu,
Seoul, South Korea, 06120
Country of Birth: United Kingdom
Family: single

ABOUT HIM:
Job now: Coffee products representative and salesmen
Job before: Coffee Republic manager in London suburbs

CAN:
- speak English and some Korean
- repair and service most commercially made coffee machines
- fully consult on almost all aspects of running a coffee shop

CAN'T:
- stand going camping
- drink cheap coffee
- drive a car

Chores: a little cleaning in apartment every day, drop off dry cleaning, go to the store, take out the trash.
Yesterday: go to work (not take out the trash, not do laundry, not do dishes)
On vacation: usually go to countries where coffee is grown to visit plantations, eat a lot of ethnic food, drink a lot of coffee and beer, do a lot of reading.
Spare time / free time: read a book, watch T.V., go to a movie, drink beer, eat out

Sofia Rossi

Gender: Female (girl)
Birthday: December 28, 1992
Age: 24
Phone number: Home 02-2827-4349
Cell: 010-2267-9876
Address: 202 Sung Eun Villa, Banpo-dong, Seocho-gu, Seoul, South Korea, 06541
Country of Birth: Italy
Family: Family is in Italy
Mom (Francesca / Birthday: September 1, 1970 / 46 years old / Clothes shop manager)
Dad (Antonio / Birthday: October 17, 1968 / 48 years old / Real estate agent).

ABOUT HER:
Job now: Barista at coffee shop / University student
Job before: University student in Rome, Italy

CAN:
- speak Italian and some English
- bake cakes and cookies
- play tennis

CAN'T:
- drive a car
- paint
- ride a bike
- speak Korean

Chores: wash dishes, do laundry, vacuum, mop the floor, iron shirts, empty trash
Yesterday: study English, go to part-time job, vacuum, read a book, (not wash dishes, not go to a restaurant, not drink)
On vacation: usually visit a new city in Korea, try local food, visit local sites, take photos
Spare time / free time: watch a movie, watch English dramas, talk to family and friends in Italy on Skype, meet friends

UNIT

1 In the Classroom

Warm-up Questions:

1) What is your name?

My name is ________ ________ ________ .

(given names) (family name)

2) Where are you from?

I am from ________________ .

(country)

3) Where do you live?

I live in ________________ .

(city)

Name Examples:
김민서 → Min Seo Kim
이민영 → Min Young Lee
권윤아 → Yoon Ah Kwon

South:
"TH" Pronunciation practice:

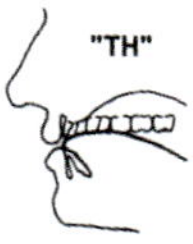

City Examples:
Seoul / Uijeongbu / Ilsan
Namyangju / Guri / Pocheon

Dialogue A:

John: Hi, Ricardo. 1. How is it going?

Ricardo: John! Hey, 2. I'm doing fine. Thanks. How about you?

John: I'm doing great. Thanks. Hey… is anyone sitting here?

Ricardo: No, no one. Please sit down. 3. Do you know Jenny?

John: No, I don't think we have met before. Hi. I'm John Ellers.

Jenny: Hi John. My name is Jenny Belfort. Are you a Tourism Major?

John: No, I'm a Computer Programming Major.

Jenny: 4. That is interesting. I have always wanted to know more about computers but I am more of a people person. So I am a Tourism Major, dealing with tourists and helping them.

John: That's cool too. 5. How are classes so far?

Jenny: They are great but there is so much to learn. I am worried.

Ricardo: She says that but she is doing really well.

Substitution Drill: Use the following responses in the above conversation. Practice each with a partner two times. Try to pronounce each word correctly.

		A	B
1.	How is it going?	What's up?	How are you today?
2.	I'm doing fine.	Nothing much.	I'm not bad.
3.	Do you know	Did you meet	Have you met
4.	That is interesting.	Good to know.	Oh, really.
5.	How are classes so far?	Are classes going okay?	How is school treating you?

CULTURAL NOTE:

There are many ways of saying the same thing in English.
The substitution drill is to give you both **more options** and **chances** to understand more fluently.

Partner Practice:

What is your name?	What is your major?	How are classes going?
My name is ________ ________ . (given name) (family name)	I am a ________ . (department)	My classes are going ________ . (good/bad/so-so)
What is your partner's name?	**What is your partner's major?**	**How are your partner's classes going?**
My partner's name is ________ ________ . (given name) (family name)	My partner is a ________ . (department)	My partner's classes are going ________ . (good/bad/so-so)

Now find a new partner and practice the answers and answers.

What is your partner's name?	What is your partner's major?	How are your partner's classes going?
My partner's name is ________ ________ . (given name) (family name)	My partner is a ________ . (department)	My partner's classes are going ________ . (good/bad/so-so)

Conversation Corner 1: *How are you?*

There are several ways to ask and answer this greeting.

QUESTION

A. How are you? today?

B. How's it going?

C. What's up?

D. How are things going?

E. How have you been?

RESPONSE

F. Good. You?

G. I'm good. Thanks. How about yourself?

H. I'm good. Thank you for asking. How about you?

I. I'm good. Thank you. And you?

J. Things are going good.

Not unlike Korean, English has a way of being more and less polite, depending on whom we are talking to. Number the questions and responses on previous page in order from most formal to least formal.

한국어와 마찬가지로 영어에도 대화 상대방에 따라 공손하게 또는 반말로 말하는 방법이 있습니다. 앞 페이지의 질문과 답변을 가장 공손한 표현에서부터 차례로 번호를 붙여보세요.

QUESTION(A-E)		RESPONSE(F-J)
1. ______	*Most Formal* 격식이 있는	1. ______
2. ______		2. ______
3. ______		3. ______
4. ______	*Least Formal* 격식이 없는	4. ______
5. ______		5. ______

Who do you speak formal and not formal to?

Formal	Not formal(informal)
Teacher	*Classmate*

Responses: *There are good and bad responses. Bad responses break the pattern of talk. Remember that "How are you?" is more of a greeting than a true question of personal feeling.

A: How are you?
B: I'm ______________ .
Thanks. And you?
A: ______________ . Thanks.

Good Response		"Bad" Response	
good	not bad	terrible	sad
so-so	fine	bad	lonely
okay	well	hungry	not good
alright	______	wonderful	busy
______	______	______	______

WHY ARE THESE "BAD"?

Practice the conversation above with several other students.

Grammar Focus 1: *Subject Pronouns, Usage.*

SUBJECT PRONOUN	USAGE	PICTOGRAM
I	• to talk about one's self Ex. I am a man. I like fruit.	

You	• to talk about second person known **Ex.** You are tall. You like oranges. • can also mean a group of people **Ex.** You are in a line.	 
He	• talks about 1 male person, present or not present **Ex.** He has a hat. He is short.	
She	• talks about 1 female person, present or not present **Ex.** She is old. She talks well.	
It	• talks about 1 non-person thing **Ex.** It is heavy. It lies on the table.	 
They	• 2+people, things, places, nouns **Ex.** They are tall. They like books.	 
We	• I and another, others **Ex.** We are fun. We like to swim.	

BOY OR GIRL?
HE OR SHE?

Boy names: ➡ HE

James	John
William	Robert
Michael	David
Richard	Charles
Ricardo	Daniel
Thomas	Chris
George	Brian
Matthew	Kevin
Eric	Peter

Girl names: ➡ SHE

Mary	Patricia
Linda	Barbara
Maria	Elizabeth
Jennifer	Susan
Dorothy	Margaret
Lisa	Betty
Karen	Nancy
Helen	Michelle
Carol	Sandra
Donna	Joann

"Subject Pronouns" take the place of nouns.

Ex. Brian goes to class at Kyungbok. Brian enjoys studying.
Brian likes to drink coffee. Brian is a good student.
→ Brian goes to class at Kyungbok. He enjoys studying.
He likes to drink coffee. He is a good student.

NOTE: All sentences start with CAPITAL or BIG letters!
모든 문장은 대문자로 시작합니다.

Exercise 1 *Circle the correct Pronoun.*

Ex. Craig	they / (he)				
1) birds	it / they	2) Susan and Joe	she / they	3) Susan	she / it
4) a balloon	it / they	5) balloons	it / they	6) a computer	it / they
7) You and I	they / we	8) Paul and Ricardo	he / they	9) Ricardo	he / they
10) a car	it / they	11) roses	it / they	12) gorillas	it / they

Exercise 2 *Replace the following nouns with an appropriate pronoun.*

a bird	*it*	Jim		Susan	
a boy		university		I+class	
2 girls		two pencils		clouds	
2 birds		I+family		you and you	
the teacher		Jim and Susan		Mom and Dad	
Paul		Paul and Harry		Harry and Paul	
a mouse		mice		a child	
children		a person		people	
the sky		your teacher		your best friends	

NOTE: Korean Language tends to drop the "subject". English does not!
Use a subject in almost every sentence when writing and speaking!
한국어는 "주어"를 생략하는 경향이 있지만 영어는 그렇지 않습니다.
글을 쓸 때나 말을 할 때 거의 모든 문장에서 주어를 사용하세요.

Exercise 3 *Find and replace the subject noun in the following sentences.*

Ex. Brian likes to play soccer. ➡ He likes to play soccer.

1. 1 bird is eating a bug.

2. 2 birds are eating a bug.

3. 3 birds are eating a bug.

4. Mom is baking.

5. Dad is eating.

6. Mom and Dad are sleeping.

7. I and Robert like soccer.

8. Robert and Susan are tired.

9. I, Robert and Susan are resting.

10. The computer is broken.

11. Nancy walks to school.

12. Chris takes a bus.

13. My university is on a hill.

14. Other person is standing.

15. English class is easy.

NOTE: Pronouns replace repetitive usage of noun names. They are important because you need to be able to follow the pronoun in a conversation.
대명사는 명사의 반복적 사용을 대체합니다. 대명사가 중요한 이유는 대화할 때 대명사를 잘 이해해야 하기 때문입니다.

Exercise 4 *Read the following. Who are the pronouns?*

A boy named Corey came to class. 1. He was tall and had long hair. 2. It was brown. 3. He sat down next to a girl named Beth. 4. She was short with black hair. 5. It was short. 6. They talked about coffee before class started. 7. They both liked coffee. The bell for class rang. When 8. it stopped, 9. they stopped talking. The next day, Corey gave Beth a coffee. 10. She was happy.

1. He: Corey	2. It: ______	3. He: ______
4. She: ______	5. It: ______	6. They: ______
7. They: ______	8. it: ______	9. they: ______
10. She: ______		

Ex. Mary is a good friend. He is easy to talk to. ✘ Mary is a good friend. She is easy to talk to. ✔

My Mom and Dad are boring. It are not fun. ✘ My Mom and Dad are boring. They are not fun. ✔

NOTE: The relationship between the subject and verb is very important. It is the source of many exam questions for this course and in TOEIC, TOEFL, and IELTS tests. It is very important that you make sure to replace with the correct pronoun.
주어와 동사의 관계는 매우 중요합니다. 본 강좌와 토익과 토플 그리고 IELTS 같은 시험에서 많이 출제되는 문제이기 때문입니다. 정확한 대명사로 확실하게 대체하는 것이 매우 중요합니다.

Exercise 5 *Look at the two people.*

- plays soccer
- likes pizza
- works at market
- studies at university
- watches T.V.

- plays tennis
- likes pizza
- works at library
- studies at university
- has a dog

Fill in the blanks below with the appropriate pronoun "He", "She", or "They".

1. ______ plays soccer.	2. ______ works in a library.	3. ______ like pizza.
4. ______ has a dog.	5. ______ works at market.	6. ______ study at university.
7. ______ watches TV.	8. ______ plays tennis.	

Exercise 6 *Follow the pronoun. When does it change?*

Every morning, I wake up at 6:15 a.m. I go to the gym. 1. It is a five minute walk from my house. I exercise until 7:45 a.m. I go home. My house is a small apartment, but 2. it is very close to many nice things. When I get home, my mom is cooking breakfast. 3. She is a great cook. I enjoy eating her meals. My sister is awake too. 4. She is younger than me, and very smart. 5. She enjoys studying everything. My father drinks coffee and reads the newspaper every morning. 6. He likes to have quiet time when 7. he reads. Then my mother reads the paper. 8. They both read the paper, but enjoy different news stories in 9. it. After I shower, 10. we all eat breakfast together. My dad and sister leave after breakfast. 11. They leave at 8:45. I leave for the bus at 9:00. I am never late, but sometimes 12. it is.

1. gym	2. ______	3. ______
4. ______	5. ______	6. ______
7. ______	8. ______	9. ______
10. ______	11. ______	12. ______

Look at Exercise 6 from the previous page. Answer the following questions.

Now compare answers 3. and 4. Are they the same or different? ______

Now compare answers 4. and 5. Are they the same or different? ______

Now compare answers 8. and 11. Are they the same or different? ______

Now compare answers 9. and 12. Are they the same or different? ______

Now compare answers 6. and 7. Are they the same or different? ______

From the above, can you make a rule for pronouns' usage?

위 내용을 보고 대명사 사용 규칙을 기술할 수 있을까요?

______

______

______

______

Dialogue B:

Professor: In English, learn about your partner and prepare to describe yourself and your partner.

Min Seo: Hello. my name's Min Seo Kim.

Julia: Hi, Min Seo. I'm Julia Strauss.
1. It is nice to meet you.
I guess we are partners.

Min Seo: Nice to meet you too, Julia.
Let's begin. Where are you from?

Julia: 2. I am from the United States.
How about you?

Min Seo: I'm from South Korea. I like America a lot though. How old are you?

Julia: 3. I'm 20 years old. You look about the same, right?

Min Seo: Actually, I'm 22 years old. Two more questions. What is your major and what kind of a student are you?

Julia: I'm a nursing major and I think 4. I'm a good student but others think that I 5. talk too much in class. How about you?

Min Seo: I'm a Computer Programming Major. I am a hard working student.

Professor: Min Seo, will you please introduce your partner to us all?

Min Seo: Everyone, this is Julia Strauss. She is from the United States.
She is 20 years old. She is a nursing major and a good student.

Substitution Drill: Use the following responses in the above conversation. Practice each with a partner two times. Try to pronounce each word correctly.

		A	B
1.	It is nice to meet you.	Nice meeting you.	Glad to meet you.
2.	I am from the United States.	I'm American.	I come from the U.S.A.
3.	I'm 20 years old.	I'm 20.	I just turned 20.
4.	I'm a good student	I study well	I am doing ok in class
5.	talk too much in class.	I am doing very well.	I am fun to sit with.

Conversation Corner 2: *Meeting new people*

Meeting new people usually means saying "Nice to meet you".
There are many ways of saying "Nice to meet you".

Conversation Point:

It is important to practice both the formal and informal forms of English. Also, often we use the corresponding answer when one person first speaks. The more formal the starter is, the more options the response has.

대화의 요령: 격식을 차린 영어와 일상영어 모두 연습하는 것이 중요합니다. 누군가 처음 말을 할 때 적절한 응답을 합니다.
대화를 시작하는 사람이 격식을 차릴수록 다양한 답변이 가능합니다.

1. A: Nice to meet you.
- B: Thank you. I'm surprised you heard of me. ✗
- B: The pleasure is all mine. ✗
- B: Nice to meet you, too. ✓
- B: Thank you. It's nice to finally meet you, too. ✓

2. A: It's a pleasure to meet you.
- B: Thank you. I'm surprised you heard of me. ✗
- B: The pleasure is all mine. ✓
- B: Nice to meet you, too. ✓
- B: Thank you. It's nice to finally meet you, too. ✓

3. A: It's an honor to meet you.
I have heard good things about you.
- B: Thank you. I'm surprised you heard of me. ✓
- B: The pleasure is all mine. ✓
- B: Nice to meet you, too. ✓
- B: Thank you. It's nice to finally meet you, too. ✓

Grammar Focus 2: *The Verb "to be", Usage and Conjugation:*

The most important verb in English, as well as many other languages, is "to be".
많은 다른 언어에서도 그렇겠지만 영어에서 가장 중요한 동사는 "be"입니다.
It has many purposes but we will focus on 1) Locative 2) Complement
많은 용법이 있지만 1) 처격(위치)과 2) 보어에만 집중해서 설명하겠습니다.
Today, we will focus on its complement form. Think of "to be" as " = "
오늘은 "be"동사의 보어형식에 국한합니다. "be"동사는 " = "로 간주하세요.

Ex. Curtis is fat Curtis = fat

Pronoun	Affirmative	Negative(not)	Question(?)
I	I am (I'm)	I am not (I'm not)	Am I... ?
You We They	You are (You're) We are (We're) They are (They're)	You are not (You aren't) We are not (We aren't) They are not (They aren't)	Are you... ? Are we... ? Are they... ?
He She It	He is (He's) She is (She's) It is (It's)	He is not (He isn't) She is not (She isn't) It is not (It isn't)	Is he... ? Is she... ? Is it... ?

Exercise 7 *Choose the correct form of the verb "to be" and fill in the blanks below.*

1. I ______________________
2. You ______________________
3. He ______________________
4. She ______________________
5. They ______________________
6. We ______________________
7. It ______________________
8. You and I ______________________
9. Susan ______________________
10. Frank ______________________
11. The computer ______________________
12. Frank and John ______________________
13. John and Susan ______________________
14. I ______________________
15. A bird ______________________
16. Birds ______________________
17. Computers ______________________
18. You ______________________
19. They ______________________
20. The teacher ______________________
21. Oranges ______________________
22. An orange ______________________
23. The erasers ______________________
24. Bill and I ______________________

TIP: The exercise above is to help you combine the last exercise and a new exercise.

1st Look at the subject and replace it with a pronoun.

2nd Put the right form of the verb in the blank.

Ex. You and I ________ *(1st "You and I" ➡ "We")

We ________ *(2nd what verb ➡ am? is? are?)

We __are__

Exercise 8 *Use the correct form of the verb in the following sentences. Use "am" "is " or "are".*

1. I ________ a student.
2. Susan ________ tall.
3. He ________ happy.
4. They ________ funny.
5. The eraser ________ dirty
6. We ________ in the class.
7. It ________ red.
8. You and I ________ short.
9. Frank ________ kind.
10. Frank and John ________ baseball players.
11. The computer ________ fast.
12. The cellphones ________ off during class.
13. The cat ________ on the T.V.
14. We ________ angry.
15. Susan and I ________ Nursing majors.
16. John ________ a teacher.
17. The bird ________ sick.
18. They ________ unhappy.
19. A cloud ________ white.
20. The students ________ tired.
21. The pencil ________ under the book.
22. She ________ pretty.
23. The man ________ outgoing.
24. The people ________ ugly.

Put the words after the "am, is, are" sentence ends from Exercise 8 into the correct box below. Questions 1-6 are done for you.

연습문제 8의 "am, is, are"로 끝나는 문장 뒷부분 다음에 있는 단어를 아래 해당하는 빈 칸에 채워 넣으세요.

Describes Appearance	# 2 tall # 5 dirty
Describes Personality	# 4 funny
Describes Feelings	# 3 happy
Describes Job	# 1 a student
Describes Location	# 6 in the class

Contraction Practice: A contraction is two words connected into one.

I am → I'm		
You are → You're	We are → We're	They are → They're
He is → He's	She is → She's	It is → it's

CAREFUL

It's → it is   Its → possessive

You are → you're   Your → possessive

NOTE: Contractions are considered low level English when written. For formal reports or assignments, avoid all contractions.

축약은 문어체 영어에서는 저급한 표현으로 간주됩니다. 공식 보고서나 과제에서는 일체 축약된 표현을 사용하지 마십시오.

Exercise 9 *Make contractions from the following sentences.*

1. He is tall. He's tall.	**2.** They are playing outside.	**3.** It is done.
4. I am thinking.	**5.** She is short.	**6.** I am tired.
7. She is thin.	**8.** We are finished.	**9.** He is funny.
10. It is a hill.	**11.** You are out-going.	**12.** She is shaking hands.
13. They are heavy.	**14.** We are hungry.	**15.** They are playing cards.
16. You are smart.	**17.** I am going home.	**18.** I am over here.

Exercise 10 *Make sentences using the contractions:*

1. (I am): ______________________________ .
2. (He is): ______________________________ .
3. (They are): ______________________________ .
4. (She is): ______________________________ .

TOEIC VOCABULARY

Read the following common TOEIC words. Memorize so that you can do well on the TOEIC. Write the Korean and English below in the blanks two times to help you learn.

beat: 물리치다, 이기다, 순찰구역.
In order to beat your competitors, you should work harder than now.
(경쟁자들을 물리치려면 지금보다 더 열심히 해야 한다.)

_________ /_________ _________ /_________

conduct: 수행하다.
Chemical experiment should be conducted with much care.
(화학 실험은 매우 조심스럽게 수행되어야 한다.)

_________ /_________ _________ /_________

lean: 기대다.
They are leaning against the wall.
(그들은 벽에 기대어 있다.)

_________ /_________ _________ /_________

stack: 쌓다.
Several bags are stacked on the table.
(가방 여러 개가 탁자 위에 쌓여 있다.)

_________ /_________ _________ /_________

suggest: 제안하다.
What does the man suggest the woman do?
(남성은 여성에게 무엇을 하라고 제안하고 있나요?)

_________ /_________ _________ /_________

decline: 거절하다.
Why did she decline his invitation?
(그녀는 왜 그의 초대를 거절했나요?)

_________ /_________ _________ /_________

help: 돕다.
What did he help her do?
(그는 그녀가 무엇을 하는 것을 도와주었습니까?)
What did he help her with?
(그는 그녀의 어떤 업무를 도와주었습니까?)

_________ /_________ _________ /_________

predict: 예측하다.
What temperature is predicted for this afternoon?
(오늘 오후는 기온이 어떨 것으로 예측됩니까?)

_________ /_________ _________ /_________

face: 마주보다, 직면하다
The car is facing the people.
(차량 한 대가 사람들을 마주하고 있다.)

_________ /_________ _________ /_________

gather: 모으다.
They gathered around the keynote speaker.
(그들은 기조연설자 주위에 모여들었다.)

_________ /_________ _________ /_________

stare: (물끄러미) 바라보다.
I'm tired of staring at the computer screen.
(컴퓨터 화면을 응시하는 것이 지겹다.)

_________ /_________ _________ /_________

mention: 언급하다.
What is not mentioned about the used goods?
(중고 물품에 관해 언급된 것이 아닌 것은 무엇입니까?)

_________ /_________ _________ /_________

describe: 설명하다.
How can the woman be described best?
(여성을 어떻게 하면 가장 잘 설명할 수 있을까요?)

_________ /_________ _________ /_________

cover: 덮다, 다루다.
How many agendas will be covered in the next seminar?
(다음 세미나에서는 몇 가지의 의제가 다루어질까요?)

_________ /_________ _________ /_________

qualify: 자격을 갖추게 하다.
What feats qualify him for this award?
(어떤 공적 덕분에 그는 이 상을 수상할 자격이 있는 것입니까?)

_________ /_________ _________ /_________

article: 기사, 물건, 관사.
What is this article mainly about?
(이 글은 주로 무엇에 관한 것인가요?)

__________ /__________ __________ /__________

urge: 독촉하다, 성화하다.
The executive urged the managers to supervise new employees properly.
(사장님은 간부직원들에게 신입직원들을 제대로 감독하라고 성화했다.)

__________ /__________ __________ /__________

place: (주문을) 하다.
If you want, I will place an order on behalf of you.
(원하시면 당신 대신 주문을 해 드리겠습니다.)
Many NGO's place great importance on health problems.
(많은 비정부기구들이 건강 문제에 상당한 의미를 부여한다.)

__________ /__________ __________ /__________

announce: 발표하다.
A new merger has been announced by the president of the company.
(신규 합병이 사장님에 의해 발표되었다.)

__________ /__________ __________ /__________

worry: 걱정하다.
What is she worried about?
(그녀는 무엇에 관해 걱정하고 있습니까?)

__________ /__________ __________ /__________

gaze: 응시하다.
She is gazing at the bulletin board.
(그녀는 게시판을 바라보고 있다.)

__________ /__________ __________ /__________

tear: 찢다, 눈물.
They are tearing the notice off the board.
(그들은 게시판에서 쪽지를 떼어내고 있다.)

__________ /__________ __________ /__________

attach: 첨부하다.
Several documents are attached to this e-mail.
(몇 가지 서류가 이메일에 첨부되어 있습니다.)

__________ /__________ __________ /__________

concern: 걱정.
I have several concerns I would like to ask you about.
(당신에게 여쭤 보고 싶은 걱정거리가 몇 가지 있습니다.)

__________ /__________ __________ /__________

sale: 판매.
The house is for sale.
(이 집을 판매합니다.)

__________ /__________ __________ /__________

customer: 고객.
Customer satisfaction department is open 24 hours a day.
(고객 만족부서는 하루 24시간 근무합니다.)

__________ /__________ __________ /__________

confidence: 자신감, 신뢰.
Many students don't have much confidence in their abilities.
(많은 학생들이 자신의 능력에 자신이 없다.)

__________ /__________ __________ /__________

guest: 손님.
The hotel is always crowded with guests enjoying their life.
(호텔은 인생을 즐기는 손님으로 항상 붐빈다.)

__________ /__________ __________ /__________

client: 고객.
I have an appointment with a very important client.
(매우 중요한 손님과 약속이 되어 있습니다.)

__________ /__________ __________ /__________

invitation: 초대, 초청장.
Why didn't you send an invitation to Julia?
(어째서 Julia에게 초청장을 보내지 않았니?)

__________ /__________ __________ /__________

schedule: 일정, 일정을 잡다.
What is the president's schedule like for this afternoon?
(오늘 오후 사장님의 일정은 무엇인가요?

__________ /__________ __________ /__________

TOEIC GRAMMAR EXERCISES:

Choose the correct answer. Some of the grammar has advanced rules. We are hoping that by exposure, we can expand on your knowledge base.

1) The team ______ ready to play baseball.
A) am B) is C) are

2) The members of the team ______ ready to play baseball.
A) am B) is C) are

3) Everybody ______ happy when the team takes the field.
A) am B) is C) are

4) All of the parcels ______ very heavy. Be careful when lifting them.
A) am B) is C) are

5) One of the parcels ______ very heavy. Be careful when lifting it.
A) am B) is C) are

6) The man ______ very scary looking.
A) am B) is C) are

7) All the birds are very pretty but I like that pink one. That one ______ my favorite.
A) am B) is C) are

8) All the birds are very pretty but I like those pink ones. Those ones ______ my favorite.
A) am B) is C) are

9) He and I ______ not a couple.
A) am B) is C) are

10) People ______ sometimes late for meetings.
A) am B) is C) are

11) Neither the goat nor the cow ______ healthy.
A) am B) is C) are

12) Both the cow and the goat ______ brown.
A) am B) is C) are

13) The increasing rate of overweight people ______ a worldwide issue.
A) am B) is C) are

14) Money ______ the root of all evil.
A) am B) is C) are

UNIT

2 Where is the... ?

Warm-up Questions:

First, from last week...

1) What is your name?

My name is ______ ______ ______.

2) Where are you from?

I am from ______________________.

3) Where do you live?

I live in ______________________.

New Questions For Today!

4) How old are you?

I'm ______________ years old.
(age)

5) When is your birthday?

My birthday is in ____________________ .
(month)

My birthday is on ____________ ____________ , ____________ .
(date) (month) (year)

> **KOREAN AGE:**
> In Korea, you are born almost a year old. However, this is not the case in most other countries. Remember, when speaking to a person from another country, your age is about 1 year LESS.
> 한국에서는 태어나자마자 거의 한 살을 먹는다. 하지만 이런 현상은 대부분의 다른 나라와 다른 것이다.
> 다른 나라에서 온 사람에게 말할 때 본인의 나이를 한 살 줄여서 말하도록 하자.

6) What is your job? What do you do?

I am a ______________ . (job)

I work part-time as a ______________ . (job)

I work part-time at ______________ . (job place)

> **JOB BANK:**
> student / server / bartender / cook / banquet hall greeter / house keeper / busperson / baker / clerk / nurse

Dialogue A: *"Where did it go?"*

Ricardo: Hmm... 1. where did it go?
John: Hey, Ricardo.
What are you looking for?
Ricardo: My pen. It was here before break.
I thought I left it 2. on my book or in my book, but it is gone.
John: Is it on the floor or in your bag?
Ricardo: No, 3. I checked both of those already.
John: What does it look like?
Ricardo: It is 4. a typical blue pen. Nothing special but it was my only pen.
John: I think I found it.
Ricardo: Really? Where?
John: Ricardo, it is behind your ear!
Ricardo: Huh? Oh... 5. I'm an idiot.
John: No, you're not. You are just having one of those days.

Substitution Drill: Use the following responses in the above conversation. Practice each with a partner two times. Try to pronounce each word correctly.

		A	B
1.	where did it go?	where is it?	where is my pen?
2.	on my book or in my book	on the desk or on my chair	somewhere around here
3.	I checked both of those already.	I already looked there.	It is not there.
4.	a typical blue pen.	silver pen with a black top.	white and blue pen.
5.	I'm an idiot.	I must be tired.	I am dumb.

CULTURAL NOTE:

In the last sentences in the dialogue, Ricardo calls himself an idiot. In American culture, as well as other English cultures, this is a common behaviour. People can call themselves bad names, but it is not appropriate for the other person to do it.

위 대화 마지막 문장에서 Ricardo는 자신을 바보라고 부른다. 다른 영어권 문화권은 물론이고 미국 문화에서도 이것은 일반적인 행동이다. 사람들은 자신을 부정적인 호칭으로 부르지만 다른 사람을 바보라고 부르는 것은 예의에 어긋난다.

John says that Ricardo is "having one of those days".
This means a bad day and implies that everyone has one. Does this exist in your culture too?

John은 Ricardo가 "having one of those days"라고 말하는데 그 의미는 운수가 나쁜 날이라는 뜻이고 누구나 당할 수 있다는 의미이다. 한국어에도 이런 표현이 있나요?

Comprehension Questions: Try to answer in complete sentences.

1. What is Ricardo "looking for"? (looking for = trying to find)

____.

2. Is the pen special?

____.

3. Where is the pen?

____.

Conversation Corner 1:

Getting to know each other. Learning how to ask questions politely.

Who are you? / Are you married? / How old are you?

Often times, Korean people ask what seems to be a correct question, but it is not polite due to its bluntness. For example, "Who are you?" is not a great way to ask another person's name in the first meetings.

종종 한국인들은 정확해 보이기는 하지만 어색함 때문에 예의에 어긋나는 질문을 한다. 예를 들면 "누구세요?"는 처음 본 사람의 이름을 물을 때 쓸 수 있는 좋은 방법은 아니다.

Title	Single	Married	? Single ? Married ?
Man	Mr. (mister)	Mr. (mister)	Mr. (mister)
Woman	Miss (miss)	Mrs. (misses)	Ms. (mizz)
Both	Doctor → Dr. / Professor → Prof. / President → Pres.		

Who are you?

Who are you? ✘ ➡ Excuse me. May I ask your name, please? ✔

Are you married?

Are you married? ✘ **Woman** ➡ Excuse me, Ms. ______________ … ? ✔

Woman: Miss ______________ . or

Woman: Mrs. ______________ or

Woman: "Yes, Ms. ______________ "

➡ Pardon me, but may I ask if you are married? ✔

For women, the answer is how they want to be called. In the case of "Ms.", many professional women like the title, including teachers and businesswomen. When meeting for the first time, or talking on the phone with an unknown woman, "Ms." is the correct title until the woman corrects it.

여성에게 정답은 그들이 불리우기를 바라는 방식에 있다. "Ms."의 경우 교사와 사업가를 포함한 많은 전문직 여성들은 이 호칭을 좋아한다. 처음 만난 사이이거나 모르는 여성에게 전화로 대화할 때 그 여성이 교정해 주지 않는 한 "Ms."가 정확한 호칭이다.

Are you married?

Are you married? ✘ **Man** ➡ Excuse me, Mr. ________ , but are you married? ✔

➡ Mr. ________ , is there a Mrs. ________ ? ✔

As the title for men is "Mr." in both cases, often men aren't asked if they are married or not.

남성의 호칭이 두 경우 모두 "Mr."이기 때문에 종종 남성들은 결혼 여부를 묻는 질문을 받지 않는다.

How old are you? ✘

In Korea, knowing the other person's age is very important for knowing how to speak to another person and what to call them. But as "형" "누나" "오빠" and "언니", don't translate in English, asking age is more delicate. **If it is not important, DON'T ASK**, especially with woman. It can be very rude to ask a woman from western cultures her age.

한국에서는 타인에게 어떻게 말하고 뭐라고 부르는가를 알기 위해 타인의 나이를 아는 것이 매우 중요하다. 하지만 "형" "누나" "오빠" 그리고 "언니"라는 개념이 영어로는 번역할 수 없기 때문에 나이를 묻는 것은 좀 민감한 사안이다. 중요하지 않으면 묻지 않는 게 좋다. 특히 여성에게는 그렇다. 서양에서 온 여성의 나이를 묻는 것은 매우 무례한 행동일 수 있다.

If you must know the age, ask as follows:

➡ "If it's not too personal, would you mind if I asked your age?" ✔

➡ "I'm sorry if this seems rude, but may I ask you your age? ✔

Talking about location

One of the many uses for "to be" is to tell where something is.

We can use "to be" with the above words "on", "above", "over", "in front of", "beside", "below", "under" and "behind" to talk about where things are.

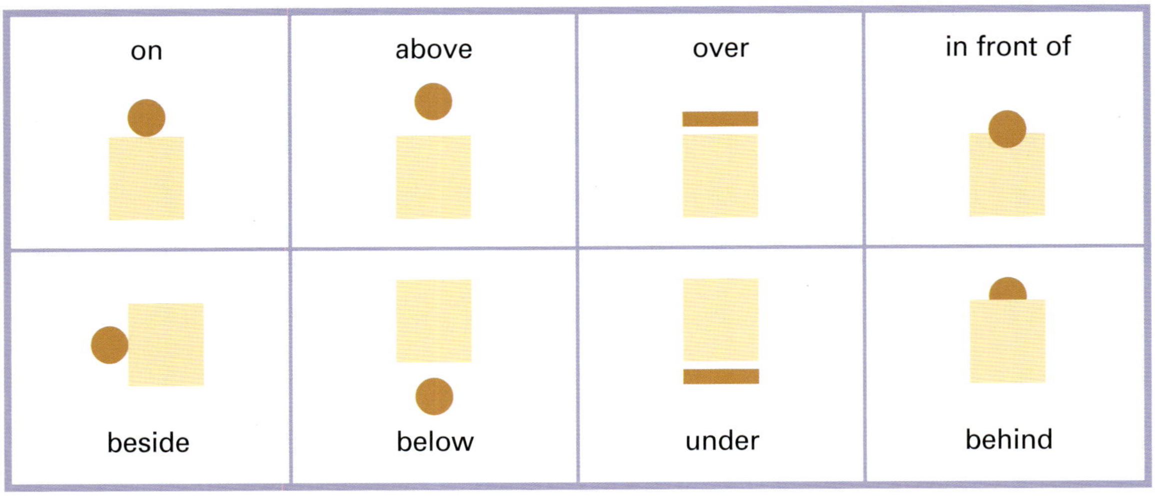

Exercise 1 *Where is the cat? Where is the dog? Circle the correct answer. The first one is done for you.*

A. The dog is: on the chair / under the chair

B. The cat is: on the table / in the table

C. The cat is: behind the computer / on the computer

D. The dog is: behind the closet / in the closet

E. The dog is: behind the bed / on the bed

F. The dog is: behind the picture / in front of the picture

G. The cat is: behind the drawer / on the drawer

H. The cat is: next to the TV / under the TV

Exercise 2 *Fill in the blanks with "to be" and "on", "above", "over", "in front of", "beside", "below", "under" and "behind".*

1. Where is the cat?
   The cat ___is beside___ the chair.
2. Where is the book?
   The book ______________ the table.
3. Where is the book?
   The book ______________ the lamp.
4. Where is the ball?
   The ball ______________ the table.
5. Where is the pillow?
   The pillow ______________ the chair.
6. Where is the clock?
   The clock ______________ the wall.
7. Where is the lamp?
   The lamp ______________ the table.
8. Where is the rug?
   The rug ______________ the table and chair.

Exercise 3 *Work with a partner. Make your own questions and answers about the picture.*

With a partner, talk about the things on your desk or in the classroom using "locative be verb".

Ex. There is a board in front of the room.
There is a board behind the professor.
There is a boy next to the window.

Dialogue B: *New Apartment*

Sofia: So, 1. what do you think of my new apartment?

Akari: Well, it's a bit small but there is a lot of natural light and there are some great restaurants nearby. When will you move your stuff in?

Sofia: 2. This weekend, I hope.
I have a plan for everything.
The T.V. and entertainment center will go over there on that wall and the study desk with computer over here. I'll put the sofa across from the T.V. The armchair can go over there and the coffee table between.

Akari: Hmm... 3. are you sure about that?

Sofia: 4. What do you mean? Is there a problem with the plan?

Akari: I have seen your furniture and I think it's too big for this room. There isn't enough space for the table and the desk. There isn't enough space for the armchair as well.

Sofia: Really? I guess I will have to put the study desk in the bedroom and armchair on the balcony.

Akari: I'm not sure if the study desk will fit in the bedroom with your queen sized bed.

Sofia: Oh no! 5. You must help me figure this out. The stuff arrives in a few days.

Akari: Relax, you can always put a few things in storage for a while. But let's see what we can do.

Substitution Drill: Use the following responses in the above conversation. Practice each with a partner two times. Try to pronounce each word correctly.

		A	B
1.	what do you think of	what is your opinion on	what is your first impression of
2.	This weekend, I hope.	This Saturday and Sunday, I hope.	It is supposed to be at the weekend.
3.	are you sure about that?	do you really think that?	are you certain that is correct?
4.	What do you mean?	Why do you ask?	I don't understand. What is the problem?
5.	You must help me figure this out.	You have to help me solve the problem.	I really need your help to fix this.

With a partner, talk about your bedroom or your apartment.
Use "There is / There are / There aren't / There isn't" sentences.

Conversation Corner 2: Goodbye

There are many different ways to say goodbye in every language.

In different situations, we use a different goodbye. Which above goodbye would be best for each situation?

여러 상황에서 서로 다른 헤어질 때의 인사법을 사용한다. 위의 인사법 가운데 다음의 상황에 가장 적합한 것은 어느 것인가?

__G__ You will continue your conversation next time.

_____ Saying casual goodbye (from Italian language).

_____ Saying goodbye at an airport (or when you will not meet soon).

_____ You are talking to a customer / professor / important person

_____ Saying goodbye at night time / end of the day (*can be said during late afternoon)

_____ You will meet your friend tomorrow.

_____ Saying goodbye to a friend.

_____ You will call your friend on the phone.

_____ Your friend is in the hospital.

Grammar Focus: *The Verb "to be" in the negative form:*

Pronoun	Affirmative	Negative(not)	Question(?)
I	I am (I'm)	I am not (I'm not)	Am I… ?
You We They	You are (You're) We are (We're) They are (They're)	You are not (You aren't) We are not (We aren't) They are not (They aren't)	Are you… ? Are we… ? Are they… ?
He She It	He is (He's) She is (She's) It is (It's)	He is not (He isn't) She is not (She isn't) It is not (It isn't)	Is he… ? Is she… ? Is it… ?

Exercise 1 *Choose the correct form of the verb "to be" in the negative form and fill in the blanks below.*

1. I ____________
2. You ____________
3. He ____________
4. She ____________
5. They ____________
6. My friend and I ____________
7. It ____________
8. You and I ____________
9. Susan ____________
10. Frank ____________
11. The computer ____________
12. Frank and John ____________
13. John and Susan ____________
14. Perth family ____________
15. A bird ____________
16. Birds ____________
17. Computers ____________
18. Your friend ____________
19. They ____________
20. The teacher ____________
21. The fork and the spoon ____________
22. We ____________
23. The erasers ____________
24. Bill and I ____________

TIP: The exercise above is to help you combine the last exercise and a new exercise.

1st Look at the subject and replace it with a pronoun.

2nd Put the right form of the verb in the blank.

Ex. John ________ *(1st "John" ➡ "He")

He ________ *(2nd "what verb ➡ am? is? are?)

He is *(3rd add "not")

He is not (4th make "contraction" IF YOU WANT. NOT NECESSARY

원하면 축약을 하지만 필요한 것은 아닙니다.

He isn't

Exercise 2 *Use the correct negative (NOT) form of the verb "to be" in the following sentences.*

1. I ________ a student.
2. Susan ________ tall.
3. He ________ happy.
4. They ________ funny.
5. The eraser ________ dirty
6. We ________ in the class.
7. It ________ red.
8. You and I ________ short.
9. Frank ________ kind.
10. Frank and John ________ baseball players.
11. The computer ________ fast.
12. The cellphones ________ off during class.
13. The cat ________ on the T.V.
14. We ________ angry.
15. Susan and I ________ Nursing majors.
16. John ________ a teacher.
17. The bird ________ sick.
18. They ________ unhappy.
19. A cloud ________ white.
20. The students ________ tired.
20. The pencil ________ under the book.
22. She ________ pretty.
23. The man ________ outgoing.
24. The people ________ ugly.

GAME TIME: TRUE OR FALSE:

Quietly write 5 sentences about yourself or your family using "am / am not / is / there is / there are". Make some sentences false and some sentences true. Then read your sentences to your partner and have them guess if they are true or false. DON'T TELL THEM IF THEY ARE FALSE OR TRUE UNTIL AFTER. Ask your teacher for help at any time. Have fun. Be interesting.

"am / am not / is / there is / there are"을 사용하여 자신 또는 자신의 가족에 관한 5개의 문장을 조용히 써 보세요. 일부 문장은 거짓말로 쓰고 일부 문장을 사실로 쓰세요. 그리고 나서 상대방에게 자신이 쓴 문장을 읽어준 뒤 참인지 거짓인지 추측하게 해 보세요. 사실인지 거짓인지 끝까지 말하지 마세요. 언제라도 교수님께 질문을 해서 도움을 받으세요. 즐기세요. 재미있게 하세요.

Ex. I think dancing is fun. (true) My father is taller than me. (false)
There are 3 T.V.s in my house. (false) There is a T.V. in my bedroom. (true)

My sentences:

1. ____ .
2. ____ .
3. ____ .
4. ____ .
5. ____ .

TOEIC VOCABULARY

Read the following common TOEIC words. Memorize so that you can do well on the TOEIC. Write the Korean and English below in the blanks two times to help you learn.

announcement: 발표.
What is the topic of this announcement?
(위 발표문의 주제는 무엇인가요?)

__________ /__________ __________ /__________

destination: 목적지.
What is the destination of this flight?
(비행의 목적지가 어디인가요?)

__________ /__________ __________ /__________

passenger: 승객.
How many of the passengers died?
(몇 명의 승객이 사망했습니까?)

__________ /__________ __________ /__________

cause: 원인, 야기시키다.
What is the suspected cause of the accident?
(사고의 원인으로 추정되는 것은 무엇입니까?)

__________ /__________ __________ /__________

exhibition: 전시, 전시회.
The world printing machine exhibition is held every two years.
(세계 인쇄기기 전시회는 2년에 한 번씩 개최됩니다.)

__________ /__________ __________ /__________

measures: 조치.
Strong measures should be introduced to increase public security.
(대중의 안전을 증진하기 위해 강력한 조치가 도입되어야 한다.)

__________ /__________ __________ /__________

renewal: 갱신.
Contract renewal should be done within this month.
(계약 갱신은 이번 달 안으로 해야 합니다.)

__________ /__________ __________ /__________

shift: 교대, 변경, 변경하다.
Why do you always get the Friday shift?
(어째서 너는 항상 금요일 근무를 하는 거냐?)

__________ /__________ __________ /__________

warranty: 품질보증.
How long is the warranty for the new product?
(신제품에 대한 품질보증 기간은 얼마인가요?)

__________ /__________ __________ /__________

objective: 목적.
What is the speaker's primary objective?
(연사의 주요 목적은 무엇입니까?)

__________ /__________ __________ /__________

transportation: 운송, 교통.
What is their best choice for transportation?
(그들의 가장 좋은 운송수단은 무엇입니까?)

__________ /__________ __________ /__________

despite: ~에도 불구하고
Despite his financial difficulty, he succeeded in starting a new company.
(재정적 어려움에도 불구하고 그는 새로운 회사 설립에 성공했다.)

__________ /__________ __________ /__________

along: ~를 따라서.
Cars are parked along the street.
(승용차 여러 대가 거리 옆에 주차되어 있다.)

__________ /__________ __________ /__________

through: ~를 통해, ~를 꿰뚫고.
He finally solved the problem through incessant endeavor.
(그는 부단한 노력을 통해 마침내 문제를 풀어냈다.)
Terrorists entered the country through the mountains.
(테러분자들이 산악을 통해 우리나라에 침투했다.)

__________ /__________ __________ /__________

inconvenience: 불편함.
I am awfully sorry for the inconvenience.
(불편을 드려 매우 죄송합니다.)

__________ /__________ __________ /__________

purpose: 목적.
What is the purpose of this notice?
(이 공지의 목적은 무엇입니까?)

__________ /__________ __________ /__________

charge: 외상.
Will you pay for this by cash or charge?
(현금인가요 아니면 카드인가요?)

__________ /__________ __________ /__________

variety: 다양함.
A variety of collection is in display in this gallery.
(이 화랑에는 다양한 작품이 전시되어 있다.)

__________ /__________ __________ /__________

estimate: 견적, 견적을 내다.
The company asked for an estimate for the air-conditioning work of the office.
(회사 측에서 사무실 냉동 공사비 견적서를 요청했습니다.)

__________ /__________ __________ /__________

retirement: 정년퇴직.
Would you like to contribute to the gift for his retirement?
(그의 정년퇴직 기념품에 기부를 하시겠습니까?)

__________ /__________ __________ /__________

venue: 장소.
Clara is looking for a new venue for the conference.
(Clara가 새로운 회의 장소를 물색하고 있습니다.)

__________ /__________ __________ /__________

on: ~위에.
What are the biggest discounts on?
(어느 상품에 가장 큰 할인이 적용됩니까?)

__________ /__________ __________ /__________

against: ~에 대항하여, ~에 반대하여.
Many people bought special insurance to prepare against the possibility of earthquake.
(지진의 가능성에 대비하기 위해 많은 사람들이 특별보험 상품을 구매했다.)

__________ /__________ __________ /__________

because of: ~때문에.
Because of the hot weather, sales of air conditioners have doubled this summer.
(더운 날씨 때문에 올 여름에 냉방기 판매가 두 배로 뛰었다.)

__________ /__________ __________ /__________

in: (장소) ~안에, (시간) ~후에.
What may happen in an hour?
(한 시간 뒤에 무슨 일이 일어날까요?)

__________ /__________ __________ /__________

within: (시간) ~이내에.
She will come back within an hour.
(그녀는 한 시간 이내에 돌아올 것이다.)

__________ /__________ __________ /__________

after: (시간) ~후에.
They came back after an hour.
(그들은 한 시간 후에 돌아왔다.)

__________ /__________ __________ /__________

over: ~에 걸쳐, ~넘어.
The company has made great contributions to the country over the past few years.
(우리 회사는 지난 수년에 걸쳐 국가에 엄청난 기여를 해 왔다.)

__________ /__________ __________ /__________

UNIT

3 Family Evening at Home

Review Questions:

- What is your name?

  My name is ______________ ______________ ______________.

- How old are you?

  I'm ______________ years old.

- What do you do?

  I'm a ______________. (I work part-time as a ______________)

Warm-up Questions:

7) Do you like your job? Why (not)?

__________ , it's __________ .
(Yes, I do/No, I don't) (adjective)

8) What does your mother/father do?

My mother is a ________ and my father is a ________ .
(job) (job)

9) How many people are in your family?

There are __________ people in my family.
(number of people, including you BUT NOT pets)

ADJECTIVE EXAMPLES:
Fun, interesting, boring, hard work, easy, long hours, far from my home, repetitive.
재미있는, 흥미로운, 지루한, 어려운 일, 쉬운, 오랜 시간, 집에서 먼, 반복적인

JOB EXAMPLES
Hair dresser 미용사
Businessman 사업가
Engineer 기술자
Cook 요리사
Waiter (식음료) 종업원
House wife(Home Maker) 가정주부

Dialogue A: *Phone Call*

Linda: Hello?
Jenny: Hello, is this Mrs. Perth?
Linda: Yes.
Jenny: Hi, Mrs. Perth, 1. my name is Jenny Belfast. 2. May I speak to John, please?
Linda: Sure, Jenny. Are you John's friend?
Jenny: Yes, 3. we go to school together.
Linda: Oh, I see. It's nice to meet you Jenny. 4. Let me call him.
……
John: Hello, Jenny? What's up?
Jenny: Hi John, not much. Hey, do you have time to answer the survey from our Spanish class?
John: Oh yes, I forgot about that… Look, I am sorry but I'm having dinner right now. Can I call you back at 9:00 p.m.?
Jenny: Oh, sorry! Sure, nine is fine! I am going out now, but you can call me on my cell phone.
John: Okay, what's your cell phone number?
Jenny: It's 010-5524-4420
John: Got it! 5. Talk to you later, Jenny.
Jenny: Bye.

Substitution Drill: Use the following responses in the above conversation. Practice each with a partner two times. Try to pronounce each word correctly.

		A	B
1.	my name is	this is	I am
2.	May I speak to John,	Is John home,	Is John available,
3.	we go to school together.	we are classmates.	I go to school with him.
4.	Let me call him.	He's right here.	I'll put him on.
5.	Talk to you later,	I'll call you later,	Talk to you soon,

Conversation Concentration: What's your phone number?

There are several ways to say phone numbers out loud in English.

- You can stop at each number:

  0 1 0 – 5 5 2 4 – 4 4 8 0

  zero one zero five five two four four four eight zero

- You can say <u>*Oh*</u> for <u>*0*</u>

  0 1 0 – 5 5 2 4 – 4 4 8 0

  oh one oh five five two four four four eight oh

- You can say two numbers together as one number (**ex.** 54 is fifty-four / 89 is eighty-nine)

  0 1 0 – 5 5 2 4 – 4 4 0 0

  oh one oh fifty-five twenty-four forty-four zero zero

- If two numbers are the same and next to each other, you can say "double"
  If three numbers are the same and next to each other, you can say "triple"

  0 1 0 – 5 5 4 4 – 4 4 4 0

  oh one oh Double five double four triple four zero

- You can mix any of the above.

  0 1 0 – 5 5 4 6 – 4 4 5 9

  oh one oh fifty-five forty-six double four five nine

The rule is: No rule! Depending on the number, you can choose whichever way is fastest, clearest, and most convenient to remember.

규칙: 정해진 규칙은 없습니다. 숫자에 따라 가장 빠르고 명확하고 가장 기억하기 편리한 방법을 택하면 됩니다.

Look at these phone numbers, decide the best way to say them out loud.

0 1 0 – 8 1 0 0 – 1 0 0 0 ______ – ______ – ______

0 2 4 – 1 0 1 0 – 2 0 2 2 ______ – ______ – ______

1 – 800 – 7 0 6 0 – 1 2 0 0 ______ – ______ – ______

2 1 3 – 5 5 5 2 – 0 0 0 2 ______ – ______ – ______

0 0 7 – 4 8 4 2 – 1 2 3 0 ______ – ______ – ______

For home phones, the first three numbers are called the ***area code***, and may be skipped if speaking to someone from the same neighborhood.

가정용 전화의 경우 첫 세 숫자는 지역번호이기 때문에 같은 지역에 사는 사람에게 전화를 걸 때는 생략할 수 있습니다.

Match. Then practice saying the following numbers together.

031 – 570 – 9707 •	• zero one zero ninety-nine fifty-five twenty- eight twenty-eight
010 – 3246 – 2878 •	• one eight hundred six four five twenty- four twenty- four
010 – 9955 – 2828 •	• one three oh six six nine two twenty-five forty-seven
1 – 306 – 692 – 2547 •	• zero one zero three two four six twenty eight- seventy eight
02 – 4576 – 8889 •	• zero one zero ninety-nine thirty- three five oh oh nine
010 – 9933 – 5009 •	• zero three one five seven zero ninety-seven oh seven
1 – 800 – 645 – 2424 •	• eighty-two ten ninety-seven oh five zero zero six zero
8210 – 9705 – 0060 •	• zero two forty five seventy six eighty-eight eighty-nine

SURVEY RACE: WHO CAN GET 10 PHONE NUMBERS FASTEST?

Name:	Phone Number:
1.	
2.	
3.	
4.	
5.	
6.	
7.	
8.	
9.	
10.	

Dialogue B: *Phone call for Dad*

John: Mom, it's Mr. Smith. He wants to talk to dad.

Linda: Well, I don't want to wake him up. He has to get up early tomorrow. Ask him if it's important.

John: Mr. Smith, my father is sleeping right now. 1. Is it okay if he calls you back in the morning?

Mr. Smith: 2. Oh sure, no problem. Could I leave a message?

John: Sure, let me get a pencil... okay, go ahead.

Mr. Smith: Please tell him Mr. Kim would like to speak with him. 3. He is available by phone anytime this week at the office or on his cell phone. Mr. Kim can be reached at the office at 031-453-4559 or on his cell phone at 010-4056-9194.

John: Okay Mr. Smith, 4. I will let him know in the morning.

Mr. Smith: Thank you. Have a good evening now.

John: 5. You, too. Mr. Smith. Bye!

Substitution Drill: Use the following responses in the above conversation. Practice each with a partner two times. Try to pronounce each word correctly.

		A	B
1.	Is it okay if he calls you back	May he call you back	Can he get back to you
2.	Oh sure, no problem.	Of course!	That would be fine.
3.	He is available	He can be reached	You can contact him
4.	I will let him know	I will tell him	I will give him the message
5.	You, too.	You as well.	So do you.

Conversation Corner: *Answering the phone / Taking a message*

Answering the phone: Write the letters (A-G) in the correct box.

- A. Hey! What's up?
- B. Hi!
- C. Yes?
- D. Good afternoon. Min speaking! How can I help you?
- E. Good afternoon! This is Min.
- F. Hello, ABC Company, how can I help you?
- G. Hello?

Your Friend is calling:	Unknown Number(?):	At work:
A.		

REMEMBER: "Hi!" is informal. "Hello" is better for formal/unknown situations.
"Hi"는 스스럼없는 표현이며 "Hello"는 격식을 갖추거나 낯선 상황에서 사용합니다.

Taking messages: The three steps to follow are important.

1. Giving reason for message	2. Getting information	3. Confirming information
A) I'm sorry but (he / she) is busy at the moment. Can I take a message? B) I'm sorry to say but (he / she) is unavailable right now. Can I take a message? C) I'm afraid that (he / she) ____________ . Can I take a message? 죄송합니다만 그 분은 지금 바쁘신데요. 전하실 말씀이 있으신가요?	A) Could I get your name and number please? B) May I have the reason for the call? C) Do you want (him / her) to call you back? A) 성함과 연락전화번호를 알려주실 수 있으신가요? B) 용건이 무엇인지 알 수 있을까요? C) 그 분이 전화드리기를 바라시나요?	A) Ok, so that is ____________ (name) from ____________ (company name) at ____________ (phone number) . You would like him / her ____________ (to call back/to know that you called) A) 네, 제이름은 ____ 이고 ____ 회사 소속 이며 전화번호는 ____ 입니다. B) 그 분이 전화를 하기를 원하시는군요. C) 그 분께 당신이 전화했다는 것을 알려 드리기를 원하시는군요.

* I'm afraid that = I'm sorry to say (유감이지만...)

PRACTICE WITH A PARTNER WITH THE FOLLOWING INFORMATION:

Mark Anderson Central University Office: 031-4545-2784 Cell: 010-8889-9010 Would like him to call back	Gillian Gilton Hotel Hotelier: John Goodman Office: 016-6831-7722 Cell: 010-7887-6008 Will call again tomorrow	"J.J." from J.J. Custom Suits 010-6454-8823 or 010-9876-8823 Come by our office at 11 Main street anytime. Your suit is ready.

Grammar Focus: *The Verb "to be", in the negative form (locative):*

Affirmative	Negative(not)	Question(?)
There is	There isn't (is not)	Is there ... ?
There are	There aren't (are not)	Are there ... ?

"There is" and There are" are used to express where things are in a space.

Singular (단수) ➡ There is a / There isn't a / Is there a... ?

Affirmative	Negative(not)	Question(?)
There is a teacher in the room.	**There isn't an** elephant in the room.	**Is there a** pencil in the room?
There is a computer in the room.	**There isn't a** marker in the room.	**Is there a** sofa in the classroom?
There is a cup on the desk.	**There isn't a** store near here.	**Is there a** washroom near here?
	*is not = isn't	

Exercise 1 *Make sentences: "There is a...", "There isn't a..." and "Is there a..." about your classroom.*

There is a ______________________________.

There is a ______________________________.

There isn't a ______________________________.

There isn't a ____ .

Is there a ____ ?

Is there a ____ ?

Plural (복수) ➡ There are (some) / There aren't / Are there any... ?

Affirmative	Negative(not)	Question(?)
There are some teachers in the room.	**There aren't any** elephants in the room.	**Are there any** pencils in the room?
There are some computers in the room.	**There aren't any** markers in the room.	**Are there any** sofas in the classroom?
There are some cups on the desk.	**There aren't any** stores near here.	**Are there any** washrooms near here?
	*are not = aren't	

Exercise 2 *Make sentences: "There are...", "There aren't any..." and "Are there any..." about your classroom.*

There are (some) ____ .

There are (some) ____ .

There aren't any ____ .

There aren't any ____ .

Are there any ____ ?

Are there any ____ ?

Make the Rule:

Now that you have made some sentences on the last page, can you guess what the following words mean and how they are used?

앞 페이지에서 몇 개의 문장을 만들어 보았으니 다음의 단어들이 의미하는 바와 그 용법을 알 수 있을 것입니다.

a/an ➡ ____

some ➡ ____

any ➡ ____

"a / an" means "1".

In English we don't say "I have 1 dog". We say "I have a dog".

"A" is used if the following word starts with a consonant sound. ➡

"An" is used is the following word starts with a vowel sound. ➡

Consonants
b, c, d, f, g, h, j, k, l, m, n, p, q, r, s, t, v, w, x, y, z

Vowels
a, e, i, o, u

NOTE: Don't just look at the letter, listen to the sound.

Ex: a MP3 ✘ an Mp3 ✔

Why? Listen to the sound.

MP3 sounds like "Emm Pee Three"

Exercise 3 *Try the following with your partner. Insert "a" or "an.*

____ orange	____ potato	____ computer	____ union
____ meeting	____ onion	____ crazy person	____ monster
____ M.T.	____ toast	____ feather	____ fat guy
____ ice cream cone	____ hiker	____ FBI case	____ dirty look
____ leg	____ balloon	____ hour	____ amazing person

CULTURAL NOTE:

Korean people often drop "a" "an" and "the" from the conversation.
They are important words that do affect meaning. Often, it is more than a grammar mistake.
Look at the following.

한국인들은 대화에서 종종 관사를 빠뜨립니다. 하지만 관사는 의미에 영향을 주는 중요한 단어입니다. 종종 문법적 오류 이상이 되기도 합니다. 다음의 사례를 보세요.

- Could you get me pencil? How many pencils? (There is no "S" so it sounds like 1, but there is no "a" so it can't be 1.)
- Could you get me a pencil? Okay (one pencil) Could you get me pencils? Okay ("s" and no "a", many pencils).

Countable (가산명사)	**Uncountable** (불가산명사)
– things that you can count (셀 수 있는 사물)	– things you can't count (셀 수 없는 사물)
ex. some fruit: an orange, oranges / a banana, bananas some vegetables: an onion, onions / a potato, some potatoes	some fruit: blueberries / grapes / some watermelon liquids: water, cola, juice cereals: rice, grain, oatmeal powders: sugar, salt, red pepper powder, flour

1(한 개) (a / an)	2+ (들) -s	No a / an / -s
IS	ARE	IS

- What is countable / uncountable?
  It is easy to think of it this way. I call it the "가락" method.
- How many fingers do you have (손가락) ?
  10 therefore ➡ countable (can count)
- How many toes do you have (발가락)?
  10 therefore ➡ countable (can count)
- How much hair do you have? (머리카락)???
  too many to count therefore ➡ uncountable (can NOT count)

Exercise 4

PUT "C" for Countable and "U" for Uncountable on the "____".
Then put the correct form of the "be verb" after the word.
The first one is done for you.

가산명사는 "C"를 불가산명사는 "U"를 밑줄 위에 쓰시오. 그리고 단어 뒤에 "be" 동사의 정확한 형태를 써 넣으시오. 첫번째 것은 예시입니다.

1. __U__ bread __is__	2. ____ rice ______	3. ____ tigers ______
4. ____ apples ______	5. ____ a car ______	6. ____ sugar ______
7. ____ an apple ______	8. ____ wine ______	9. ____ a glass ______
10. ____ beans ______	11. ____ cars ______	12. ____ an egg ______
13. ____ kim chi ______	14. ____ juice ______	15. ____ a fried egg ______

Exercise 5

Choose the correct form of the verb "to be" in the negative (NOT) form and fill in the blanks below.
(HINT: You must decide if the object is countable or uncountable)
"be" 동사 부정형의 정확한 형태를 골라서 아래 빈 칸에 채워넣으시오.
(힌트: 목적어가 가산명사인지 불가산명사인지를 정하면 됩니다.)

1. There __isn't__ any bread.
2. There ______ any water.
3. There ______ any pears.
4. There ______ any coffee left.
5. There ______ much juice in the fridge.
6. There ______ much time before class.
7. There ______ many of these berries left.
8. There ______ many tigers in the world.
9. There ______ any tigers left in Korea.
10. There ______ much ice cream.
11. There ______ any clouds in the sky.
12. There ______ much wind today.
13. There ______ any of that blue paint left.
14. There ______ any houses for sale.
15. There ______ enough rice for both of us.
16. There ______ enough ink in the printer.

Exercise 6

Write "some" or "any" in the following blanks.

1. There are ______ apples.
2. There aren't ______ apples.
3. Are there ______ apples?
4. Is there ______ coffee?*
5. There isn't ______ coffee.*
6. There is ______ tea.*
7. There aren't ______ almonds?
8. Are there ______ walnuts?
9. Is there ______ rice?*
11. There isn't ______ rice.*
11. There are ______ peaches,
    but there aren't ______ bowls.
12. Are there ______ cups?

*In these cases, we can use "is" because liquid and rice are UNCOUNTABLE.

Exercise 7

PUT IT ALL TOGETHER: Use "a", "an", "some", "any".

1. There is ________ apple.
2. There aren't ________ apples.
3. Is there ________ apple?
4. There is ________ coffee.
5. There isn't ________ juice.
6. There are ________ cups.
7. There is ________ almond.
8. Are there ________ bananas?
9. There are ________ potatoes.
10. There isn't ________ rice.

TOEIC VOCABULARY

Read the following common TOEIC words. Memorize so that you can do well on the TOEIC. Write the Korean and English below in the blanks two times to help you learn.

since: 이후로, ~때문에.
I have not seen him since he departed.
(그가 떠난 이후르 그를 못 봤다.)
Since I love her, I will marry her.
(그녀를 사랑하기 때문에 그녀와 결혼할 것이다.)

__________ /__________ __________ /__________

therefore: 그러므로
They analyzed the initial crisis; therefore, they were able to prevent further crisis.
(그들은 초기의 위기를 분석하였다; 그 결과 추가 위기를 예방할 수 있었다.)

__________ /__________ __________ /__________

otherwise: 그렇지 않으면.
Try not to lose what you have now; otherwise, you will lose what you will have in the future.
(지금 가지고 있는 것을 잃지 않기 위해 애를 쓰세요; 그렇지 않으면 미래에 가질 수 있는 것을 잃을 것입니다.)

__________ /__________ __________ /__________

though (although, even though): 비록 ~하지만.
Although the food was excellent, I was not satisfied with the attitude of the waiters.
(음식은 훌륭했지만 종업원들의 태도는 불만족스러웠습니다.)

__________ /__________ __________ /__________

as if: 마치 ~인 것처럼.
He speaks as if he knew everything.
(그는 모든 것을 다 알고 있는 것처럼 말한다.)

__________ /__________ __________ /__________

whether: ~인지 아닌지.
I wonder whether you could visit us sometime next week.
(다음 주에 저희를 방문해 주실 수 있는지 궁금합니다.)

__________ /__________ __________ /__________

due: 지급일이 된, ~할 예정인, 당연히 해야 할.
When is the next payment due?
(다음 납부 마감일이 언제인가요?)

__________ /__________ __________ /__________

parallel: 평행의.
The bicycle is parallel to the fence.
(자전거가 벽에 나란히 서 있다.)

__________ /__________ __________ /__________

eligible: 적합한.
Who is eligible for this position?
(이 직책에는 누가 적합한가요?)

__________ /__________ __________ /__________

ago: ~전에.
University graduates were able to find decent jobs 10 years ago.
(대학 졸업자들은 10년 전에는 좋은 일자리를 구할 수 있었다.)

__________ /__________ __________ /__________

before: ~전에, 예전에.
Where has the gentleman met her before?
(신사는 그녀를 전에 어디에서 만났습니까?)

__________ /__________ __________ /__________

must: (의무의 뜻을 나타내는 조동사) 해야 한다.
You must obey your parents.
(부모님에게 복종해야 한다.)

__________ /__________ __________ /__________

have to: (목적의 의미를 강조하는 조동사) ~해야 한다.
You have to study hard in order to succeed.
(성공하기 위해서는 열심히 공부해야 한다.)

__________ /__________ __________ /__________

should (ought to): (강한 권고를 나타내는 조동사) 해야 한다.
You should go home right away to have a rest.
(쉬기 위해 즉시 집에 가라)

__________ /__________ __________ /__________

unless: ~하지 않으면 (if … not)
Unless you meet her now, you will regret in the future.
(지금 그녀를 만나지 않으면 미래에 후회할 것입니다.)

__________ /__________ __________ /__________

as: ~와 같이.
The annual health check will take place as follows:
(연례 신체검사는 다음과 같이 진행합니다:)

_________ /_________ _________ /_________

while: ~하는 동안.
I fell asleep while I was watching the movie.
(영화를 보다가 잠이 들었다.)

_________ /_________ _________ /_________

famous: 유명한.
What is this place famous for?
(이 지역은 무엇으로 유명합니까?)

_________ /_________ _________ /_________

initial: 초기의, 약자.
All the new employees must attend their initial training by next Thursday.
(모든 신입사원은 다음 주 목요일까지 초기 교육에 참여해야 한다.)

_________ /_________ _________ /_________

outstanding: 우수한, 탁월한.
His achievement was very outstanding compared to that of his competitor.
(그의 업적은 경쟁자의 업적에 비해 매우 탁월했다.)

_________ /_________ _________ /_________

technical: 기술적인.
All the technical data are included in this disc.
(모든 기술 자료는 이 디스크에 담겨있다.)

_________ /_________ _________ /_________

fraudulent: 사기성의.
The president couldn't understand the conditions and terms of the fraudulent contract.
(사장님은 그 사기 계약의 조건을 이해할 수가 없었다.)

_________ /_________ _________ /_________

would: (권유하는 표현의 조동사).
Would you like a drink?
(음료수 좀 드시겠습니까?)

_________ /_________ _________ /_________

shall: (허락을 구하는 표현의 조동사)
Shall I reprint the chart?
(도표를 인쇄할까요?)

_________ /_________ _________ /_________

will: (불확실한 미래를 가리키는 조동사)
Who will lead the workshop tonight?
(오늘 밤 교육훈련을 누가 인도합니까?)

_________ /_________ _________ /_________

look forward to: 기대하다.
We look forward to your quick reply.
(신속한 답변을 기대합니다.)

_________ /_________ _________ /_________

used to: (과거에) ~하곤 했었다.
There used be a big tree in front of the school.
(학교 앞에 큰 나무 한 그루가 있었다.)

_________ /_________ _________ /_________

be used to: ~에 익숙한.
All of us are used to this situation.
(우리 모두는 이런 상황에 익숙해 있다.)

_________ /_________ _________ /_________

object to: 반대하다.
Citizens objected to the plan of building a new city hall.
(시민들은 새로운 시청 건축 계획에 반대했다.)

_________ /_________ _________ /_________

be subject to: ~하기 쉬운.
The price is subject to change without prior notice.
(가격은 사전 통지 없이 바뀔 수 있다.)

_________ /_________ _________ /_________

TOEIC GRAMMAR EXERCISES:

Choose the correct answer. Some of the grammar has advanced rules. We are hoping that by exposure, we can expand on your knowledge base.

1) Something ______ wrong here.
A) is B) are
C) aren't D) am

2) The men ______ getting along well.
Maybe we should separate them.
A) is B) are
C) aren't D) isn't

3) There ______ some rice on the table.
Please feel free to eat it.
A) is B) are
C) aren't D) am

4) There aren't any clean bowls ______ the cupboard.
A) between B) across to
C) in D) in front to

5) There ______ any tomatoes for the pasta.
Let's go eat out instead.
A) isn't B) are
C) aren't D) am not

6) ______ there an egg to fry?
I like to eat eggs with my rice.
A) Is B) Are
C) Aren't D) Am

7) There ______ any juice.
Would you mind going and getting some?
A) is B) are
C) aren't D) isn't

8) There are too many cars ______ the road today.
We are in a traffic jam!
A) in B) above
C) across from D) on

9) Can you see if there ______ any cartons of milk?
A) are B) is
C) isn't D) am not

10) Is there ______ apple?
A) a B) an
C) any D) some

11) I think I lost my mp3.
Have you seen ______ mp3 around here?
A) a B) an
C) any D) some

12) Don't drink ______ apple juice. It has gone bad.
A) a B) an
C) the D) isn't

13) ______ there ______ apple?
A) Are / any B) Is / some
C) Are / some D) Is / an

14) Ham and cheese ______ my favorite sandwich.
A) are B) is
C) am D) aren't

15) My friend and his girlfriend ______ coming tonight.
They are both very sick.
A) isn't B) are
C) aren't D) is

UNIT

4 Professions, Hobbies and Goals

Review Questions:

- Where are you from?

  I'm from ____________ ____________.

- When is your birthday?

  My birthday is on ____________ ____________, ____________.

- Do you like your job?____________, I ____________.

  My job is very ____________________.

Warm-up Questions:

10) What do you want to be in the future? What is your dream job?

I want be a ____________________ .

My dream job is to be a/an ____________________ .

JOB LIST:

Nurse Flight Attendant Hair Stylist Office Worker Businessman Hotelier
Hospital administrator Architect Artist Computer Programmer

11) What do you like doing in your free time?

I like ____________________ (verb+ing) in my free time.

12) What are your hobbies?

My hobby is ____________________ (verb+ing) .

My hobbies are ____________________ (verb+ing) and ____________________ (verb+ing) .

Hobbies / In my free time...

swimming dancing playing computer games reading books
drinking coffee with friends hanging out with friends watching T.V.
going to the movie theater hiking playing soccer (other sports) surfing the internet

Now Practice with a partner

Professions: Use the below word box and match the professions to their pictures.

A. Programmer	B. Teacher	C. Businessman	D. Musician
E. Therapist	F. Nurse	G. Hair Stylist	H. Flight Attendant
I. Dental Hygienist	J. Web Designer		

Hobbies: Use "is" or "are" and write what hobby is going on in each picture.

______________	______________	______________	______________

Your Turn: Complete the following sentences.

1. My father is a/an ______________ . His hobby is ______________ .
2. My mother is a/an ______________ . Her hobby is ______________ .
3. My friend is a/an ______________ . His/her hobby is ______________ .
4. I am a/an ______________ . My hobby is ______________ .

Dialogue A: *The Waiting Game*

Akari: This line is long. We are going to wait for 1. quite a while.

John: I don't mind waiting. Let's pass the time by playing 20 questions.

Akari: Is that the game where you think of something and then I have to ask questions until I figure it out?

John: 2. Yes, it is. It is a fun game to pass the time. I'll go first. (pause) OK, I'm ready.

Akari: Is it a person?

John: Yes, it is.

Akari: Is the person in our class?

John: Yes, the person is in our class.

Akari: Is the person 3. a woman?

John: Yes, she is.

Akari: 4. Is she from Italy?

John: *(Sigh)* Yes, she is.

Akari: I knew it. It's Sofia Rossi. You are always looking at her. You like her!

John: Well... I think she is cute, but I haven't met her yet.

Akari: I will introduce you to her next class.

John: Really? Thanks Akari. 5. You rock!

Substitution Drill: Use the following responses in the above conversation. Practice each with a partner two times. Try to pronounce each word correctly.

		A	B
1.	quite a while.	some time.	a long time.
2.	Yes, it is.	That's right.	You're correct.
3.	a woman?	female?	a lady?
4.	Is she from Italy?	Is she Italian?	Does she come from Italy?
5.	You rock!	You are wonderful!	You are the best!

Conversation Corner 1: *Asking people to repeat themselves*

Examples of rude questions:	Examples of polite questions:
• Hey, what do you do? 이봐요, 직업이 뭐죠? • What's your job? 당신의 직업은 무엇입니까? • You swim? 수영할 줄 아세요?	• Could I ask what your job is? 직업이 무엇인지 여쭤봐도 될까요? • May I ask what you do? 무엇을 하시는지 여쭤봐도 될까요? • Do you like to swim? 수영 좋아하세요? • You look very fit. Do you swim in your free-time? 건강해 보이네요. 여가시간에 수영하세요?

Basic Rules: 1) Longer sentences are better
2) Questions beginning with: "Could" "Would" "May" are very POLITE.
("Could", "Would", "May"로 시작하는 질문은 공손한 질문입니다.)

A BIT RUDE (FINE FOR FRIENDS) *MORE POLITE*

NOTICE: The polite expressions are longer and harder to say. But it is important to learn how to speak to all sorts of people in English, just like in Korean.
공손한 표현은 길고 말하기 어렵습니다. 하지만 한국어로 말할 때와 똑같이 영어에서도 모든 종류의 사람들에게 어떻게 말하는가를 배우는 것은 중요합니다.

Let's practice. Take messages and if you need your partner to repeat what they are saying, practice the POLITE questions. 전하는 말을 들은 뒤 당신이 반복하는 것을 상대방이 원하면 정중한 질문을 연습해 보세요.

TAKE A MESSAGE (PART II)

George Hently ABC SOAP Company Office: 031-5567-1977 Cell: 010-9944-9010 Would like you to call back	Ms. Lebane. Office: 016-1112-5776 Cell: 010-9955-2828 Needs you to call after the weekend.	Jeff from Bob's Movers 010-9444-2424 Wonders if moving Saturday morning at 8:30 is still ok?

Grammar Focus: *"to be" verb and "Yes / No" questions*

Pronoun	Affirmative	Negative(not)	Question(?)	
I	I am (I'm)	I am not (I'm not)	Am I…?	Yes, you are. No, you are not. (No, you aren't.)
You	You are (You're)	You are not (You aren't)	Are you…?	Yes, I am. No, I am not. (No, I'm not.)
We	We are (We're)	We are not (We aren't)	Are we…?	Yes, we are. No, we are not. (No, we aren't.)
They	They are (They're)	They are not (They aren't)	Are they…?	Yes, they are. No, they are not. (No, they aren't.)
He	He is (He's)	He is not (He isn't)	Is he…?	Yes, he is. No, he is not. (No, he isn't.)
She	She is (She's)	She is not (She isn't)	Is she…?	Yes, she is. No, she is not. (No, she isn't.)
It	It is (It's)	It is not (It isn't)	Is it…?	Yes, it is. No, it is not. (No, it isn't.)

NOTE: To make questions with "to be", you must move the "to be" verb in front of the subject and add the question mark "?"

"be" 동사를 사용하여 의문문을 만들려면 "be" 동사를 주어의 앞에 배치하고 물음표를 첨가해야 합니다.

Some verbs that move to the front of subject to make a question: 의문문을 만들 때 주어의 앞에 써야 하는 동사들
be (am is are / was were), can / could, will / would, shall / should

Exercise 1 *Yes / No Questions: Answer the following with the correct pronoun and verb "to be".*

Ex. Are you tired? ➡ No, I'm not. / Is he tired? ➡ Yes, he is.

1. Are you a teacher?
   No, ______________________ .
2. Is he a teacher?
   No, ______________________ .
3. Are they tourism majors?
   Yes, ______________________ .
4. Is she beautiful?
   Yes, ______________________ .
5. Is Joseph tall?
   No, ______________________ .
6. Is Susan short?
   No, ______________________ .
7. Are Joe and Susan a couple?
   No, ______________________ .
8. Are you a sports fan?
   Yes, ______________________ .
9. Are we good students?
   Yes, ______________________ .
10. Is it quiet in there?
    No, ______________________ .
11. Are the computers off?
    No, ______________________ .
12. Is an apple tasty?
    Yes, ______________________ .
13. Are the apples rotten?
    No, ______________________ .
14. Is Diane a singer?
    Yes, ______________________ .

Exercise 2 *Now look at the questions in Exercise number 2. Now practice making "Yes / No Questions"*

Ex. You are happy. ➡ Are you happy?

1. The books are heavy. ______________________ ?
2. The computers are broken. ______________________ ?
3. It is dark outside ______________________ ?
4. The monkey is hungry. ______________________ ?
5. Jason is handsome. ______________________ ?
6. Sarah and Bob are waiting. ______________________ ?
7. I am thirsty. ______________ ?* ______________ ?

*(two answers possible)

8. We are on a soccer team. ______________________________ ?

9. She is near the window. ______________________________ ?

10. You are doing great. ______________ ?* ______________ ?

Exercise 3 *Look at the people below in the pictures and answer the questions.*

Are they flight attendants? ______________	Is she a hair stylist? ______________	Is he a programmer? ______________
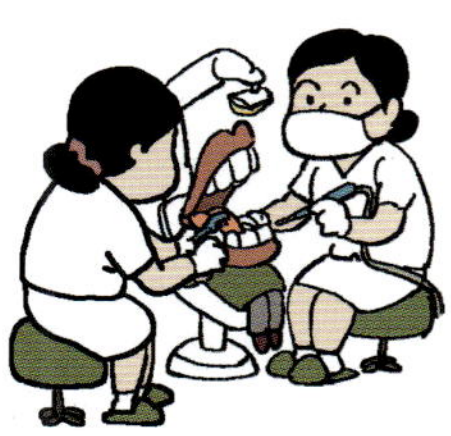		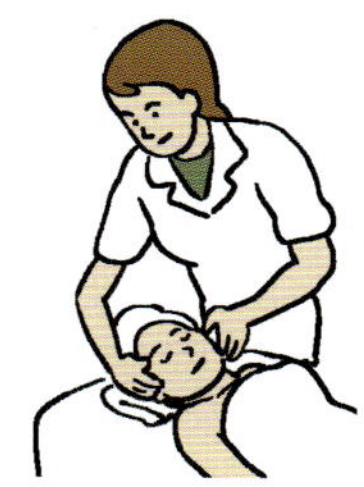
Are they dental hygienists? ______________	Is he a teacher? ______________	Is she a therapist? ______________

Is she a web designer? ______________	Is he a musician? ______________	Is she a nurse? ______________

Ask each other:
Now ask your classmates about their majors, their age, and their job.

Are you a ________ major? Yes, I am. / No, I'm not. I'm a ________ major.

Are you 23 years old? Yes, I am. / No, I'm not. I am ________ years old.

Is your birthday in June? Yes, it is. / No, it isn't. It is in ________ .

Conversation Corner: Ordinal Numbers

HERE ARE THE ORDINAL NUMBERS WITH SPELLING

1st (first)	11th (eleventh)	21st (twenty-first)	40th (fortieth)
2nd (second)	12th (twelfth)	22nd (twenty-second)	50th (fiftieth)
3rd (third)	13th (thirteenth)	23rd (twenty-third)	60th (sixtieth)
4th (fourth)	14th (fourteenth)	24th (twenty-fourth)	70th (seventieth)
5th (fifth)	15th (fifteenth)	25th (twenty-fifth)	80th (eightieth)
6th (sixth)	16th (sixteenth)	26th (twenty-sixth)	90th (ninetieth)
7th (seventh)	17th (seventeenth)	27th (twenty-seventh)	100th (hundredth)
8th (eighth)	18th (eighteenth)	28th (twenty-eighth)	
9th (ninth)	19th (nineteenth)	29th (twenty-ninth)	
10th (tenth)	20th (twentieth)	30th (thirtieth)	

1st **ex.** 21st, 31st of July	First	**ex.** The wedding will be on July 31st. Used with all DATES ending in 1 BUT NOT 11(11th).
2nd **ex.** 2nd or 22nd Floor	Second	**ex.** I live on the 22nd floor. Used with all FLOORS ending in 2 BUT NOT 12(12th).
3rd **ex.** 3rd place	Third	**ex.** The 3rd place runner won a bronze medal. Used with all POSITIONS ending in 3 BUT NOT 13(13th).
4th **ex.** 44th street	Fourth	**ex.** My friend lives on 44th street. Used with all STREET NUMBERS 4-20 / 24-30 / 34-40...

Calendar Exercise:
Write in the dates of this month using "st", "nd", "rd", and "th" correctly.

Then answer correctly by pronouncing the ordinal number correctly according to your teacher's questions.

THIS MONTH: ______________________

Sunday	Monday	Tuesday	Wednesday	Thursday	Friday	Saturday

Dialogue B:

Professor: Jenny, is this your homework?

Jenny: Yes, it is. I'm sorry professor but 1. I'm running late. Is there something wrong?

Professor: No, there isn't. You forgot to put your name on it and I wanted to 2. make sure it was you. You seem in a hurry. Are you hoping to make the next bus?

Jenny: Yes, I am. 3. I have to work then I'm going out with friends tonight.

Professor: What are you going to do with them?

Jenny: We are going to a movie tonight.

Professor: 4. Oh really. My wife and I are going to a movie tonight too. Where are you going to see it?

Jenny: We are going to the 63 Building Imax.

Professor: When are you hoping to see the movie?

Jenny: Oh, I think we are going to a show around 9 o'clock.

Professor: That is later than my wife and I like to watch movies. Have a great time and remember to review this homework and study hard.

Jenny: Yes, professor. I will. 5. Have a good day.

Substitution Drill: Use the following responses in the above conversation. Practice each with a partner two times. Try to pronounce each word correctly.

		A	B
1.	I'm running late.	I'm in a hurry.	I have a next appointment.
2.	make sure it was you.	confirm that it was yours.	be certain it was your work.
3.	I have to work	I must do a shift at work first	I am expected at work soon
4.	Oh really.	That's interesting!	Sounds fun!
5.	Have a good day.	Thank you and have a good evening.	Good night and I'll see you at next week's lecture.

Dialogue Debrief

1. Is Ellen a student? A. Yes, she is. B. No, she isn't.	**2.** Is the homework Ellen's? A. Yes, it is. B. No, it isn't.	**3.** What is Ellen doing tonight? A. She is going out with friends. B. She is going to study.
4. Where is Ellen going? A. She is going to the 63 Building. B. She is going to a park.	**5.** When is Ellen going to meet her friends? A. She is going to meet them tomorrow. B. She is going to meet them tonight.	**6.** Is Ellen going to review her homework? A. Yes, she is. B. No, she isn't.

Grammar Focus:

Using "what", "when", "where", "why", "who", and "how" with the verb "to be" (WWWWW and H")

QUESTION INFORMATION

What: used for things and objects, general nouns

a pencil — a computer
monster — monkeys
sunglasses — sports

____
____

Where: used for places, location of things in space

the park — classroom
Myungdong — café
home — Canada
department store

____
____

Who: refers to a person or people

the teacher — Sandy
those people — the workers
students — the nurse

____
____

Why: the reason behind a statement, usually with "because"

...because she was in love
...because I felt hungry
...because the moon was rising
...because I heard a noise

____
____

When: time, date an event happens

6 o'clock — last night
yesterday — this morning
September 4th, 2012
two weeks ago — tomorrow

____
____

How: used to describe a series of actions, events

with a screwdriver
in a fry pan
sliced into small pieces
carefully removing the seal

____
____

1) When making a question, the first thing you must decide is what kind of information (or answer) you want.
의문문을 만들 때 우선 결정해야 하는 것은 어떤 종류의 정보(또는 답)을 원하는가이다.

2) Decide which of the "WWWWWH" gets you that information and put it at the beginning of the sentence.
의문사 가운데 어느 것이 당신에게 그 정보를 가져다 줄 지를 결정하고 그것을 문장의 앞에 배치시키시오.

3) Is there a subject (I YOU WE THEY HE SHE IT)?
주어가 있는가를 확인하고

4) Place the correct form of the "to be" verb BEFORE the subject.
"be"동사의 정확한 형태를 주어 앞에 배치시키시오.

Ex. **1.** answer: a **place** **2.** question: **where** **3. Where** ...... you? **4.** Where are you?

Subject

Exercise 4 *Draw a line from the answer to the correct question*

1. What: •
2. Who: •
3. Where: •
4. When: • → e
5. Why: •
6. How: • → m

• a. my classmate
• b. a circle
• c. put the two pieces of bread in the toaster for about 1 minute
• d. in my home
• e. last night
• f. because it was dark
• g. mother
• h. on the rollercoaster
• i. barnyard
• j. Stephen
• k. because the monkey was hurt
• l. this morning
• m. spread the peanut butter on the slice of bread

Exercise 5 *Unscramble to make questions with the words below.*

Ex. he/what/is/playing/ ➡ What is he playing?

1. she/is/where/going/

_______________________________?

2. How/you/doing/today/are/

_______________________________?

3. at 12 o'clock/they/meeting/where/are/

_______________________________?

4. is/what/that/in the corner/

_______________________________?

5. are/that/why/you/doing/

_______________________________?

6. I/am/who

_______________________________?

7. you/staying/are/where/

_______________________________?

8. watching/what/he/is/

_______________________________?

9. they/working/together/are/why/

_______________________________?

10. is/where/feeding/the boy/puppies/

_______________________________?

Exercise 6 *Make questions from the underlined parts of the answer.*

Ex. Why is she at home? ➡ She is at home <u>because she is sick.</u>

1. _______________________________?

She is coming here <u>at 10 o'clock.</u>

2. _______________________________?

He is <u>at the library.</u>

3. _______________________________?

They are <u>my new pencils.</u>

4. _______________________________?

They are angry <u>because they have to go home.</u>

5. _______________________________?

She is <u>my new teacher.</u>

6. _______________________________?

It is wearing <u>shoes.</u>

7. _______________________________?

I am <u>in the classroom right now.</u>

8. _______________________________?

They are studying <u>carefully.</u>

9. _______________________________?

It is <u>my homework.</u>

10. _______________________________?

The party is <u>at 7 p.m.</u>

11. ______________________________ ?

We are going to the beach.

12. ______________________________ ?

I am fine. Thank you.

13. ______________________________ ?

The study group is next Monday.

14. ______________________________ ?

She is dating with the new boy in class.

15. ______________________________ ?

I am tired because I work part-time.

16. ______________________________ ?

We are doing well in English class.

Exercise 7 *Your turn: You make 3 WWWWWH questions and ask them to your partner.*

1. ____ .

2. ____ .

3. ____ .

TOEIC VOCABULARY

Read the following common TOEIC words. Memorize so that you can do well on the TOEIC. Write the Korean and English below in the blanks two times to help you learn.

turn down: 거절하다.
He turned down my proposal.
(그는 나의 제안을 거절했다.)

turn out: 내쫓다.
They turned out the beggar.
(그들은 거지를 내쫓았다.)

turn out to be: ~로 판명되다..
The assumption turned out to be true in the end.
(그 가정은 마침내 사실인 것으로 판명되었다.)

put on: 입다.
He is putting on the pants.
(그가 바지를 입고 있다.) 〈동작〉

wear: 착용하고 있다.
He is wearing the pants.
(그가 바지를 입고 있다.) 〈상태〉

take over: 인수하다.
Who will take over Stephen's job?
(누가 Stephen의 업무를 승계할 것입니까?)

take place: 발생하다.
How often does the division meeting take place?
(부서 모임은 얼마나 자주 있습니까?)

have been: (상태의 현재완료 표현)
How long have you been a medical doctor?
(의사가 되신 지 얼마나 되셨습니까?)

put up with: 참다.
You must not put up with such insult.
(이런 모욕을 참아서는 안 된다.)

come up with: 기발한 생각을 해내다.
He always comes up with a good idea.
(그는 언제나 좋은 생각을 해 낸다.)

keep up with: 보조를 맞추다.
You have to struggle to keep up with your colleagues.
(동료들과 보조를 맞추기 위해 노력해야 한다.)

catch up with: 따라가다.
Finally, I was able to catch up with the forerunners.
(마침내 선두주자들을 따라잡을 수 있었다.)

look for: 찾다.
They are looking for an experienced accountant.
(그들은 경험 있는 회계사를 찾고 있다.)

be interested in: 관심이 있다.
If you are interested in this position, please send a resume with a photo and recommendation from a former employer.
(이 직책에 관심이 있으면 사진과 이전 근무지에서 받은 추천서를 첨부한 이력서를 보내세요.)

due to (owing to): ~때문에
There was a traffic jam due to an accident.
(사고 때문에 교통 정체가 있었다.)

look over: 검토하다.
Shall I look over the document?
(서류를 검토해 볼까요?)

__________ /__________ __________ /__________

how about: (권유의 표현) ~할까?
How about trying the new restaurant?
(새로 개업한 식당에 가 보는 게 어때?)

__________ /__________ __________ /__________

what for: ~때문에.
What did the man call the lady for?
(남자가 여자에게 전화를 한 이유는 무엇인가요?)

__________ /__________ __________ /__________

what ~ like: 어떻습니까?
What's the weather like today?
(오늘 날씨가 어떤가요?)

__________ /__________ __________ /__________

how come: 어째서?
How come did she meet him again?
(어째서 그녀가 그 남자를 다시 만났습니까?)

__________ /__________ __________ /__________

be going to: ~할 예정이다.
What is he going to do tonight?
(그는 오늘 밤 무엇을 할 예정인가요?)

__________ /__________ __________ /__________

be likely to: ~할 것 같다.
Where is flooding likely to happen?
(어디에서 홍수가 발생할 것 같습니까?)

__________ /__________ __________ /__________

be due to: ~할 예정이다.
She is due to deliver a lecture on marketing.
(그녀가 마케팅에 관한 강연을 할 예정이다.)

__________ /__________ __________ /__________

be set to: ~할 계획이다.
The company is set to close all the branch offices around the country.
(우리 회사는 전국에 걸쳐있는 모든 지사를 폐쇄할 계 획이다.)

__________ /__________ __________ /__________

in advance: 미리미리
You had better reserve in advance to secure a seat.
(좌석을 확보하기 위해 사전에 예약을 하는 게 좋다.)

__________ /__________ __________ /__________

go over: 검토하다.
When should we go over the final figures?
(최종 수치를 언제 검토해야 합니까?)

__________ /__________ __________ /__________

take effect: 효력을 발하다.
When will the new rates take effect?
(새 요금은 언제부터 적용되나요?)

__________ /__________ __________ /__________

hold good: 유효하다.
This law will hold good until this year.
(이 법령은 올해까지 유효합니다.)

__________ /__________ __________ /__________

as of: 현재.
There were 100 victims as of last night.
(어제 밤 현재 100명의 희생자가 발생했다.)

__________ /__________ __________ /__________

as for: ~에 대하여 말하자면.
As for me, I am against the plan.
(내 입장을 말하면 나는 그 계획에 반대한다.)

__________ /__________ __________ /__________

as to: ~에 대하여
I didn't know as to who to meet first.
(누구를 먼저 만나야 할 지 몰랐다.)

__________ /__________ __________ /__________

UNIT

5 Going to Places and Doing Things

Review Questions:

- What is your dream job?

  My dream job is to be a/an ______________________________ .

- What do you like doing in your free time?

  In my free time, I like to ______________________________ .
  (verb)

- What does your father do?

  My father is a/an ______________________________ .

Warm-up Questions:

13) What do you like to do?

I like to ____________________.

I like to:
listen to music
sing songs
drink coffee with friends
text message on the phone

14) What kinds of things do you not like to do?

I don't like to ____________________.

I don't like to:
play the piano
ride a bicycle
watch movies
dance in Hongdae

15) What are your skills?

My best skills are ____________________.

My best skills are:
playing the piano
riding a bicycle
scoring a goal in soccer
building model airplanes

What are you good at?

I am good at ____________________.

I'm good at:
math and science
scuba diving
making sandwiches

Dialogue A:

James: Jeff, how is it going?

Jeff: 1. Can't complain. I am just thinking about what to do today.

James: Joe and I were just talking about the same thing. The weatherman is forecasting a beautiful, sunny day. Do you want to go on a bike ride with us?

Jeff: Sure, sounds like a plan. Where do you feel like riding?

James: Well, Joe and I 2. thought about riding the Hongjecheon-gil Road.

Jeff: It's a great ride! I did it last fall. The ride has an amazing mountain view and several stops for taking a break.

James: 3. Hold on a sec! I got another call on the other line.

……

James: Hello?

Joe: Hey, it's Joe, again. I am just wondering when you would like to meet.

James: 4. Why don't we say 1 ish? Jeff might come along, too. I'll tell him too.

Joe: Cool, 5. talk to you later.

Substitution Drill: Use the following responses in the above conversation. Practice each with a partner two times. Try to pronounce each word correctly.

		A	B
1.	Can't complain.	Things are pretty good.	Life is fair.
2.	thought about	decided on	are planning on
3.	Hold on a sec!	Wait a moment!	Stay put for a second!
4.	Why don't we say 1 ish?	How about 1 o'clock?	Does 1 sound good?
5.	talk to you later.	take care.	talk soon.

Partner Practice: find a partner and practice these conversations.

What do you feel like doing tonight? I feel like ____________ . (activity) *What does your partner feel like doing?* My partner feels like ____________ . (activity) *activity → watching a movie / sleeping / drinking some beer	*What is your favorite activity?* My favorite activity is ____________ . (activity) *What is your partner's favorite activity?* My partner's favorite activity is ____________ . (activity)

Conversation Corner 1: *Making Invitations (polite / impolite)*

An invitation takes the form of three structures: making invitations, accepting invitations, and declining invitations. We will concentrate on making invitations now, and look at accepting and declining invitations later.

초대에는 세 가지의 구조가 있는데 초대하기, 초대를 수락하기 그리고 초대를 거절하는 것입니다. 지금은 초대하는 것에 집중하고 초대의 수락과 거절은 나중에 다룰 것입니다.

"How about" is almost always followed by the -ing form.
"How about meeting at..."
"How about watching a movie at..."

Practice the following invitation and responses.
Then make your own invitation with your own activity.

다음의 초대와 답변을 연습하세요. 그런 뒤 활동내용을 생각해서 여러분 자신의 초대의 문장을 만들어 보세요.

Informal		Specific Invitation	Formal		Specific Invitation
Are you up for...	➡ ➡	watching a movie tonight? (your activity)	Would you like to...	➡ ➡	watch a movie tonight? (your activity)
How about...	➡ ➡	coming for dinner at our place tonight? (your activity)	Perhaps you would like to...	➡ ➡	come for dinner at our place tonight? (your activity)
Why not come around for...	➡ ➡	a piece of cake later? (your activity)	Would you care to...	➡ ➡	come to my place for a piece of cake later? (your activity)

Grammar Focus: *Present Continuous 'AM / IS / ARE' (Verb) + ING (NOW)*

In English and many other languages, including Korean, the verb is changed to reflect time. This is called "tense". Often, the time word is unnecessary because the verb "tense" tells the listener the time.

영어 그리고 한국어를 포함한 다른 언어에서 동사는 시간을 반영하기 위해 변화합니다. 이것을 "시제"라고 부릅니다. 종종 시간을 가리키는 단어는 불필요한데 그 이유는 동사의 "시제"가 듣는 이에게 시간을 말해주기 때문입니다.

For example: I **am** read**ing** a book right now. ➡ I **am** read**ing** a book.
(means "now". Listener understands "now" without it being said
because AM / IS / ARE ➡ (verb) +ING = now.)

Today's Focus is ***Present Continuous.***

*using "to play"

Pronoun	Affirmative	Negative	Yes/No Question	
I	am (verb)ing *am playing	am not (verb)ing *am not playing	Am I (verb)ing?	Yes, I am. (Yes, you are.) No, I am not. (No, you are not.)
You We They	are (verb)ing *are playing	are not (verb)ing *are not playing *aren't playing	Are you / we / they (verb)ing?	Yes, you are. No, you are not.
He She It	is (verb)ing *is playing	is not (verb)ing *is not playing *isn't playing	Is he / she / it (verb)ing?	Yes, he is. No, he is not.

Exercise 1 *Circle the correct answer in each phrase below. The first one is done for you.*

1. You ______ (is dancing / **are dancing**) very well now.
2. I ______ (are listening / am listening) to the teacher just now.
3. We ______ (is going / are going) to the theatre right now.
4. It ______ (am waiting / is waiting) outside at the moment.
5. He ______ (is playing / are playing) tennis tonight.
6. She ______ (am acting / is acting) in a group this weekend.
7. We ______ (am studying / are studying) right now.
8. They ______ (am walking / are walking) to school now.
9. I ______ (am reading / are reading) a great book these days.

Look at exercise 1. At the end of each sentence in 1-10, there are "time words". Write down the time words from the previous exercise below, and then make a rule for when to use the "Present Continuous".

1. now
2. ______
3. ______
4. ______
5. ______
6. ______
7. ______
8. ______
9. ______

When do we use the "Present Continuous Tense"?

**RULE: ______

SPELLING IS IMPORTANT!

Adding +ing to some verbs is not that easy. There are several rules to help you spell these words correctly.

NOTE: MOST WORDS ARE JUST "+ING"

Ex. play + ing = playing　eat + ing = eating　drink + ing = drinking
go + ing = going　walk + ing = walking　study + ing = studying
read + ing = reading　wait + ing = waiting　do + ing = doing

Exceptions:

1) Last letter "e" (silent "e"): If the word's last letter is an "e", you can remove the "e" before adding "+ ing".
Ex. write + ing = writing　come + ing = coming　bake + ing = baking
ride + ing = riding　hope + ing = hoping　make + ing = making
**Words ending in two "ee"s, just + ing:*
see + ing = seeing　agree + ing = agreeing　flee + ing =fleeing

2) For short vowel sound words, you double the last letter.
SHORT VOWEL SOUND → "a" in apple, "e" in bet, "i" in hit, "o" in lot, "u" in bug
Ex. run + ing = running　jog + ing = jogging　swim + ing = swimming

3) Last letters "ie": If the last letters of the word are "ie", then you change "ie" to "y"
Ex. lie + ing = lying　tie + ing = tying　die + ing = dying

Exercise 2 *Check your spelling:*

1. bleed: ______　2. give: ______
3. create: ______　4. lie: ______
5. sit: ______　6. start: ______
7. drip: ______　8. try: ______
9. take: ______　10. break: ______
11. tape: ______　12. tap: ______

Exercise 3 *Using the prompts, rearrange the words to make a sentence in the present continuous tense. You need to add "AM", "IS", "ARE" on your own.*

Ex. It / rain / today ➡ It's raining today.

1. he/study/for science quiz

_______________________________.

2. We/walk/to school

_______________________________.

3. I/have/fun time

_______________________________.

4. The train/come/in 5 minutes

_______________________________.

5. She/wear/gold earrings/

_______________________________.

6. They/wait/for the subway

_______________________________.

7. He/plan his date/with Maria

_______________________________.

8. I/read comic books/tonight

_______________________________.

9. We/drive/to the airport/right now

_______________________________.

10. You/write/the answers

_______________________________.

Exercise 4 *Using Contractions Review:*

The "present continuous" uses the verb "to be" and another verb(+ing). But the contractions we learned in Unit 2 apply here as well. Circle the words that can be contracted and write the contraction below. The first one is done for you.

> NOTE:
> "Not" usually goes on verb.
> So "We aren't" is preferred over "We're not".

1. We (are not) going to the store right now.

↓

We aren't going to the store right now.

2. (They are) playing soccer right now.

____

3. I am not studying French at the moment.

____

4. You are not watching a movie right now.

____

5. He is dancing with Cindy just now.

____

6. He is not working hard today.

____

7. We are going to the mountain this weekend.

____

8. I am not fighting with my boyfriend these days.

9. She is not walking in the park right now.

10. You are running now.

11. They are not sleeping well right now.

12. She is making cookies in the kitchen right now.

13. This weekend, it is going to be hot.

Exercise 5 *Find the mistakes.*

HINT: AM IS ARE ➡ ING

1. I am walk to the store now.
   I am walking to the store now.
2. You is being weird.
3. You are walking not on the road.
4. He are sitting in the class at the moment.
5. He is not dance with his girlfriend.
6. You aren't sit down.
7. You practice the piano this evening.
8. They's working this weekend.
9. Shen't hitting the ball right now.
10. You're are playing computer right now.

PRESENT CONTINUOUS Time words (signal words):

Present (now)	Future (little bit)
now	this evening (오늘 저녁)
right now	this afternoon (오늘 오후)
at present	this morning (오늘 아침)
currently	tomorrow (내일)
at the moment	this weekend (이번 주말)
nowadays	next… (다음…)
just now	

This is a good list to memorize for the TOEIC test.
TOEIC 시험 대비용으로 외우면 도움이 되는 도표입니다.

It is important to understand the signal word and time words because verbs in the WRONG TENSE often confuse people in regard to time. As well, the TOEIC Reading Section Part 5 "Incomplete Sentences" may give signal words as the only hints to how to answer the question. Consider the example below:

1) The messenger __________ the package at reception right now.
A) dropped off
B) is dropping off
C) drops off
D) has been dropping off

To answer this question, you must look for a signal word. In this case, it is "right now". "right now" means AM / IS / ARE → ING. So, the answer is "B" because it has "IS" and "ING"!!

Exercise 6 *The present continuous is only used for action verbs. With a partner, look at the list of verbs and circle the verbs that you think have "action":*

HINT: There are 18 action verbs!!

kick	love ✘	like	kiss	sleep	dance
go	hear	listen	look	see	understand
hate	promise	watch	make	come	walk
work	need	want	know	believe	do
play	study	hit	sit	have	punch

Look at the above verbs:
Can you find something in common with the non-action verbs.

NON ACTION VERBS are usually FEELINGS (♥) or MENTAL (🧠) verbs.

SO → If there is NO action, there is NO "to be" +ing.

I am loving you. ✘	You are needing coffee. ✘	She is seeing the cat. ✘
I love you. ✔	You need coffee. ✔	She sees the act. ✔

NOTE: "SEE" AND "HEAR":
In English "see" and "hear" are considered unintentional. There is no action in it.
영어에서 "see"와 "hear"는 의도가 없는 것으로 간주됩니다. 행위가 없는 것이지요.

NON ACTION		ACTION	
see	ex. I see something ahead. ✔ I am seeing something ahead. ✘	look watch	ex. I am looking at the picture. ✔ I am watching a soccer match. ✔
hear	ex. I hear a strange noise. ✔ I am hearing a strange noise. ✘	listen	ex. I am listening to music. ✔

Practice with a partner:
Write 3 things you are doing right now and 3 things your partner is doing right now... Make sure to use the proper spelling and to use only action verbs.

WHAT ARE YOU DOING RIGHT NOW?

1. ______________________________
2. ______________________________
3. ______________________________

WHAT IS YOUR PARTNER DOING RIGHT NOW?

1. ______________________________
2. ______________________________
3. ______________________________

Dialogue B:

Sarah: Maria, what are you doing on Saturday night?

Maria: I 1. have no plans now. What's happening?

Sarah: How about joining Nancy and I for dinner and drinks?

Maria: 2. Fantastic idea. Work has been busy recently, and I really need a night out.

Sarah: So, Nancy knows a little lounge she thinks is great. The food is great and the drinks cost 3. next to nothing. Do you know where the Korean Rock and Roll hall of fame is? It's next to it, on the right, called "Two Glasses".

Maria: Nancy always knows the good places. What time should I be there?

Sarah: Well, why don't we pick you up around 7 o'clock? One more thing, Maria. Nancy is going through kind of a rough time lately. I think we should do something nice for her.

Maria: Oh, 4. I'm sorry to hear this. How about surprising her with tickets for next month's jazz festival?

Sarah: Great thinking! That will totally 5. lift her spirits.

Substitution Drill: Use the following responses in the above conversation. Practice each with a partner two times. Try to pronounce each word correctly.

		A	B
1.	have no plans	don't have anything planned	have a clear schedule
2.	Fantastic idea.	Good thinking.	What a great idea!
3.	next to nothing.	really cheap.	cheaper than most other places.
4.	I'm sorry to hear this.	This is unfortunate news.	How terrible!
5.	lift her spirits.	make her feel better.	make her smile again.

Comprehension Questions:

1. What is Sarah doing? She ________ Maria.

   A) call　　B) is calling

   C) calling　　D) is

2. When are they planning on having a "night out"?

   A) Tonight at 7 o'clock　　B) Saturday after work

   C) Saturday at 7 o'clock　　D) Next month

3. How is Nancy feeling these days?

   A) sad　　B) tired

   C) happy　　D) hungry

4. Which is NOT a reason "Two Glasses" a good place to meet?

   A) the food is good　　B) the drinks are cheap

   C) Nancy likes it　　D) Rock and Roll Hall of Fame play there.

Conversation Corner 2: *Accepting / declining invitations*

What follows is formal and informal ways of accepting an invitation.

Accepting Invitations (초청 수락하기)	
Formal	Informal
We'd like very much the opportunity to...	I'm in.
What a delightful idea. I'd love...	Sounds like a plan.
It will be my pleasure to attend.	Sure, I look forward to it

Speaking Tip:
After accepting an invitation, it is customary to ask "Is there something I can bring?"

What the following table shows is formal and informal ways of declining an invitation. It is important to be polite when you decline an invitation. People normally say they're sorry they can't accept the invitation, and give a reason why they cannot do something / go out somewhere.
다음 도표에 나오는 표현은 초청을 거절하는 격식이 있는(없는) 표현입니다. 초청을 거절할 때에는 정중해야 합니다. 일반적으로 초청을 수락할 수 없어서 미안하다는 말을 한 뒤 무엇인가를 할 수 없거나 어딘엔가를 갈 수 없는 이유를 밝히면 됩니다.

"I'm sorry I can't make the invitation, but…"

Declining Invitations

Formal	Informal	Reasons
That's very kind of you to offer, but…	I can't.	I have to work early tomorrow.
It sounds delightful, but…	This evening is no good.	I have an appointment.
Unfortunately, I am unable to make it because…	Bad timing.	I already have plans.
I'm afraid it won't be possible, as…	I don't think it will work today.	I'm meeting friends a little later.

Practice with a partner.
Practice saying "yes" and "no" to the following activities.

- invite your professor over for a fancy dinner next week
- invite a friend out for a few beers
- invite a potential client to have lunch with you. You will pay the bill.
- invite your brother or sister over for a barbecue. He / she should bring some meat.

Exercise 7 *Make the present continuous:*

1. (he/walk to school now) He's walking to school now.
2. (I/study at the moment) ______
3. (I/not/sleep) ______
4. (you/not/play soccer tonight) ______
5. (they/read) ______
6. (she/not/work today) ______

7. (he/not/wait for the bus) ______________________

8. (we/watch T.V.) ______________________

9. (she/eat kimchi) ______________________

10. (you/not/read the newspaper) ______________________

11. (we/not/go to the movies) ______________________

12. (I/not/live in Suwon) ______________________

13. (we/study English) ______________________

14. (they/not/leave now) ______________________

15. (they/not/live in Busan) ______________________

Exercise 8 *Partner work: Interview a partner with one of the questions below.*

(Partner name) ______________ , what are you doing now?

1. Now, ______________________ .
2. At the moment, ______________________ .
3. Right now, ______________________ .

(Different Partner) ______________ , what are you NOT doing right now?

1. (Not) Now, ______________________ .
2. (Not) At the moment, ______________________ .
3. (Not) Right now, ______________________ .

(Different Partner) ______________ , what are you doing tonight?

1. Tonight, ______________________ .
2. This evening, ______________________ .
3. This weekend, ______________________ .

TOEIC VOCABULARY

Read the following common TOEIC words. Memorize so that you can do well on the TOEIC. Write the Korean and English below in the blanks two times to help you learn.

competitor: 경쟁업체, 경쟁자.
The company has better products than its competitors.
(그 회사는 경쟁업체보다 더 나은 제품을 생산한다.)

_________ /_________ _________ /_________

product: 결과물, 제품.
Low morale among the work force is the product of bad management.
(직원들 사이의 사기가 낮은 이유는 경영을 잘못한 결과물이다.)

_________ /_________ _________ /_________

employee: 종업원.
The boss has fired many employees for their low performance.
(사장은 실적이 낮은 많은 직원들을 해고했다.)

_________ /_________ _________ /_________

factory: 공장.
Many workers are gathering around the gate of the factory.
(많은 직원들이 공장 정문 근처로 모여들고 있다.)

_________ /_________ _________ /_________

market: 시장.
The gold market is steady. Prices are not changing much.
(금 시장은 안정되어 있다. 가격이 급격히 변하지 않는다.)

_________ /_________ _________ /_________

customer: 손님.
Customer satisfaction is our priority among others.
(고객 만족이야말로 다른 것들 가운데 가장 중요한 것이다.)

_________ /_________ _________ /_________

sales: 매출액.
Sales figures have shown a slow increase compared to last year.
(작년과 비교할 때 매출액이 서서히 증가세를 보이고 있다.)

_________ /_________ _________ /_________

head office: 본사.
The head office has moved to the downtown Seoul.
(본사를 서울 시내로 옮겼다.)

_________ /_________ _________ /_________

turnover: 총 거래액.
The company has an annual turnover of 30 million dollars.
(그 회사는 3천만 달러의 연 매출액을 기록하고 있다.)

_________ /_________ _________ /_________

market share: 시장 점유율.
Several companies are trying to enlarge their market share.
(몇 개 기업이 시장 점유율을 늘리기 위해 애쓰고 있다.)

_________ /_________ _________ /_________

subsidiary: 부차적인, 보조적인.
The question of finance is subsidiary to the question of the survival of the project.
(재정 문제는 사업의 존속 문제보다 부차적이다.)

_________ /_________ _________ /_________

outlet: 판매점, 출구.
This cosmetics company has more than 100 outlets across the country.
(이 화장품 회사는 전국적으로 100개 이상의 판매점을 운영하고 있다.)

_________ /_________ _________ /_________

departure: 출국, 출발.
Many people gather around the departure sign.
(많은 사람들이 출국 신호판 근처에 모여 있다.)

_________ /_________ _________ /_________

confirm: 확인하다.
You need to confirm your flight reservation before departure.
(출발하기 전 항공편 예약을 확인할 필요가 있다.)

_________ /_________ _________ /_________

research: 연구.
Scientific research doesn't always bear fruit.
(과학적 연구가 항상 결실은 맺는 것은 아니다.)

__________ /__________ __________ /__________

produce: 농산물.
It says on the bottle "Produce of Italy."
(병에 이태리 농산물이라고 쓰여 있다.)

__________ /__________ __________ /__________

grow: 성장하다.
You must invest if you want your business to grow.
(사업이 성장하기를 바라면 투자를 해야 한다.)

__________ /__________ __________ /__________

sell: 팔다.
It is not price but quality that sells our goods.
(우리 제품이 판매되는 것은 가격 때문이 아니라 품질 덕분이야.)

__________ /__________ __________ /__________

accountant: 회계원.
The role of accountant in a small company is critical.
(소규모 회사에는 회계원의 역할은 매우 중요하다.)

__________ /__________ __________ /__________

manufacture: 대량생산하다.
The company began to manufacture the goods in question.
(회사는 문제의 그 제품을 대량으로 생산하기 시작했다.)

__________ /__________ __________ /__________

recruit: 신입사원, 채용하다.
The recruits are full of hope for their future.
(신입사원들은 미래에 대한 희망으로 가득 차 있다.)

__________ /__________ __________ /__________

secretary: 비서.
Some people think that my secretary runs the company.
(어떤 사람들은 내 비서가 회사를 운영하는 것으로 생각한다.)

__________ /__________ __________ /__________

responsible: 책임을 진.
The board of directors is responsible for anything related to the management of the company.
(이사회는 회사 운영과 관련된 모든 것에 책임이 있다.)

__________ /__________ __________ /__________

confident: 확신이 있는.
The workers were confident of the quality of their product.
(직원들은 그들의 제품 품질에 확신이 있었다.)

__________ /__________ __________ /__________

document: 서류.
Legal documents are kept in a drawer.
(법률 서류들은 서랍에 보관되어 있다.)

__________ /__________ __________ /__________

article: 제품.
Articles of clothing include socks, shirts, hats and coats.
(의류 제품에는 양말, 셔츠, 모자 그리고 코트가 포함된다.)

__________ /__________ __________ /__________

application: 지원(서).
Application form should be submitted no later than Friday.
(지원서는 금요일까지는 제출해야 한다.)

__________ /__________ __________ /__________

curriculum vitae: 이력서.
Curriculum vitae is what shows who you are.
(이력서는 당신이 누구인지를 보여주는 서류이다.)

__________ /__________ __________ /__________

representative: 대표자.
Several representatives of large companies have attended the conference.
(여러 대기업 대표자들이 회의에 참가해 있다.)

__________ /__________ __________ /__________

TOEIC GRAMMAR EXERCISES:

Choose the correct answer. Some of the grammar has advanced rules.
We are hoping that by exposure, we can expand on your knowledge base.

1) Where is the reception being held?
   A) In the Korea First Hotel banquet room.
   B) We are supposed to be there around 7:00 p.m.
   C) Receptions are fun. I can't wait.
   D) I am going to go with Mr. Brinth.

2) Where ______ the dogs?
   A) aren't B) are
   C) isn't D) is

3) What ______ the dog doing right now?
   A) aren't B) are
   C) isn't D) is

4) Why is she late?
   A) She is a fast worker.
   B) Because the elevator is broken and she is taking the stairs.
   C) She ate turkey.
   D) I'm not late. I am here on time.

5) A: ______ is the Q & A?
   B: It is after the main speech
   A) Where B) When
   C) What D) How long

6) Is the Goodman file on your desk?
   A) The file cabinet is over there.
   B) No, it isn't.
   C) Yes, the file is well written.
   D) My desk is in the room next to staff room.

7) They ______ at the moment.
   Can you call back later?
   A) eating B) eat
   C) are eating D) is eating

8) She usually drives to work but today she ______ the bus because of the rain.
   A) are taking B) takes
   C) is taking D) take

9) At the moment, I ______ K-pop.
   A) am loving B) love
   C) is loving D) are loving

10) Are the musicians ready to start the concert?
   A) No, they aren't. They are still on the bus.
   B) Yes, they are all musicians.
   C) The concert director is very picky.
   D) Musicians are people who play music for a living.

11) Who is waiting for the report on the dental equipment?
   A) It is on the second floor, across from the elevator.
   B) The dentist is taking a trip out of the country right now.
   C) There is a lot of equipment involved in construction.
   D) Mr. Cross is. Please hurry.

12) Do you want to have a quick bite to eat after we finish this next page? I am starving.
   A) The next page is a difficult one.
   B) When I was young, a dog bit me.
   C) Sure, I'm in.
   D) I am not quick since I hurt my ankle.

13) A: ______ for her birthday?
   B: She's going out to eat with her family.
   A) When is B) What is she doing
   C) Why is she eating D) How long is she doing

14) They ______ baseball today. It is raining.
   A) is playing B) isn't playing
   C) are not playing D) aren't loving

15) What ______ she ______ ?
   B) That is kimchi. It is a Korean spicy side dish.
   A) is / eating B) is / eat
   C) are / eating D) are / riding

UNIT 1-5 REVIEW

Warm-up Questions:

1. What is your name? My name is ________ ________ ________ .
2. Where are you from? I am from ________ .
3. Where do you live? I live in ________ .
4. How old are you? I'm ________ years old.
5. When is your birthday? My birthday is in ________ .

   My birthday is on ________ ________ , ________ .
6. What is your job? What do you do? I am a/an ________ .

   I work part-time as a/an ________ .
7. Do you like your job? Why (not)? ________ , it's ________ .
8. What does your mother/father do? My mother is a/an ________ and

   my father is a/an ________ .
9. How many people are in your family? There are ________ people in my family.
10. What do you want to be in the future? I want to be a/an ________ .

    What is your dream job? My dream job is to be a/an ________ .
11. What do you like doing in your free time? I like ________ in my free time.
12. What are your hobbies? My hobby is ________ .

    My hobbies are ________ and ________ .
13. What do you like to do? I like to ________ .
14. What kinds of things do you not like to do?I don't like to ________ .
15. What are your skills? My best skills are ________ .

    What are you good at? I am good at ________ .

Conversation Corner:

Exercise 1 *ORDER the sentences with ORDINAL NUMBERS (1st, 2nd, 3rd, 4th, 5th…). The first two are done for you. Blue is BOY. Pink is GIRL.*

문장을 서수로 순서를 정해 보세요. 첫 두 문제는 예시입니다. 파란색은 남자고 핑크색은 여자입니다.

_____ I would love to have coffee with you later. Let me give you my number and you can call or text me.

_____ I'm well. Thank you, and yourself?

__1st__ Hello, I'm Ricardo. It is nice to finally meet you.

__2nd__ Hello, Ricardo. I'm Sophie. It's nice to meet you too. I have heard a lot about you from John.

_____ I'm fine but I'm also a bit busy. But I hate to run off right after finally meeting you.

_____ OK. My number is 0-1-0 5-5-5-6 4-5-6-4

_____ That's ok. I'm busy too. Perhaps we can meet for coffee later?

_____ Could you repeat the last 4 numbers, please?

_____ Really? I hope everything John said was good.

_____ Yes, the last four numbers are 4-5-6-4.

_____ OK. I have your number. I'll text you later. Have a good day!

_____ Thanks. Goodbye.

_____ Sounds good. I'm ready for your number.

_____ Yes, it was all good. How are you doing today?

Exercise 2 *Respond to the following questions FOR YOU.*
You can look back in the book to each chapter if necessary.

1. How are you today? I'm ________ . Thanks. ________ ________ ?
2. Nice to meet you. Nice to ________ you, ________________
3. Would you like to go to a movie with me tonight?

   Yes, that ________________ .

   I'm sorry but I ________________ .

   I can't ________________ tonight.
4. What floor do you live on? I live on the ________________ floor.
5. Excuse me, but may I ask how old you are?

   No problem. I am ________________ old.
6. Can you give me your phone number?

   Sure, my phone number ________ ________ ________
7. Good night. Thank you. Have a ________________, too.

New Grammar: CAN / CAN'T

In English, "can" is used for talking about ABILITY and asking for something (REQUEST).

Ex. Can you swim? ABILITY ⬅ today's focus

Can you buy me some bread? REQUEST

Can ➡ abilities (할 수 있다) Can not = can't ➡ (할 수 없다)

Pronoun	Positive(+ve)	Negative(-ve) Not	Question(?)
I	can	cannot / can't	Can { I / you / we / they... / he / she / it } ?
You	can	cannot / can't	
We	can	cannot / can't	
They	can	cannot / can't	
He	can	cannot / can't	
She	can	cannot / can't	
It	can	cannot / can't	

NOTICE: There is *NO* "he / she / it' ➡ s"

Exercise 1 *Complete the sentence about YOURSELF and a partner using "can" or "can't"*

YOURSELF	PARTNER
I ________ cook pasta.	He / She ________ cook pasta.
I ________ type on a computer well.	____ ____ type on a computer well.
I ________ swim.	____ ____ swim.
I can ________________ .	________ can ________ .
I can ________________ .	________ can ________ .
I can't ________________ .	________ can't ________ .
I can't ________________ .	________ can't ________ .

Exercise 2 *Who do you know that can... ?*
Think about who you know and what they can do.

1. Who can cook kimchi tsigae? ________________
2. Who can run fast? ________________
3. Who can do hot yoga? ________________
4. Who can get 100% in English? ________________
5. Who can drive a car? ________________
6. Who can ride a motorcycle? ________________

Grammar Focus: Review

Exercise 1 *Complete the following exercises with the correct form of the verb "be".*

1. He ________ ugly.
2. Joan and I ________ going home.
3. The monkeys ________ noisy.
4. The plane ________ late.
5. The bike ________ from my father.
6. The people ________ noisy.
7. An egg ________ white and yellow.
8. John, Mike and Bo ________ sick.
9. Rome ________ the capital city of Italy.
10. Beans ________ green.

11. The poster ________ from John.

12. *Nobody ________ here.

Nobody / Everybody / Somebody	is

Exercise 2 *Circle the correct answer.*

1. There is / There are ten people in the bus.
2. There is / There are a little cat behind the tree.
3. There is / There are lots of books in the library.
4. There is / There are nobody at home.
5. There is / There are a book on the table.
6. There is / There are children in the classroom.
7. There is / There are peaches in the bowl.
8. There is / There are rice on the table.
9. There is / There are sugar in the coffee.
10. There is / There are nothing to eat in the fridge.

Exercise 3 *Fill in the blanks with "There is" or "There are".*

1. ______________________ something wrong with my ear.
2. ______________________ a frog near the lake.
3. ______________________ some flowers in the vase.
4. ______________________ some rice in the bowl.
5. ______________________ money in my pocket.
6. ______________________ some apples in the basket.

Nothing / Everything / Something / Anything	is

Exercise 4

Fill in the blanks with the correct expressions.
Use each answer 2 times!

Is there | there is | there aren't | Are there | there are | there isn't

1. Is there any milk?	No, ________ .	7. ________ any rice?	No, there isn't
2. ________ any cookies?	Yes, there are.	8. Is there a banana?	Yes, ________ .
3. Is there an apple?	Yes, ________ .	9. Are there any potatoes?	No, ________ .
4. Are there any apples?	Yes, ________ .	10. Are there any peaches?	Yes, ________ .
5. ________ any water?	Yes, there is.	11. ________ any bananas?	Yes, there are.
6. Are there any oranges?	No, ________ .	12. Is there an orange?	No, ________ .

Exercise 5

Now make answers for the questions with the answers.
Work with a partner.

1. Where is he? (at home)

   He is at home ________________ .

2. When is the movie? (at 7 p.m.)

   The movie ________________ .

3. Why are you here? (because I am tired)

   I am ________________ .

4. Where is she now? (at yoga)

   ________________ .

5. What are they? (roses)

   ________________ .

6. Why is there so much kimbab? (for the picnic)

   ________________ .

7. Who is that? (Susan)

   ________________ .

8. When is his turn? (next Saturday)

   ________________ .

TALKING TIME: INTERVIEW 2 OTHER STUDENTS

QUESTION	Name:	Name:
1. How many T.V.'s in your home?	There ______ .	There ______ .
2. Is there a T.V. where you sleep?	Yes, there is. No, there isn't.	Yes, there is. No, there isn't.
3. How many pets in your house?	There ______ .	There ______ .
4. Are there any posters on the wall of your bedroom?	Yes, there are. No, there aren't.	Yes, there is. No, there isn't.
5. Is there any cola in your fridge?	Yes, there are. No, there aren't.	Yes, there is. No, there isn't.
6. Is there a Hoolala Chicken near your home?	Yes, there are. No, there aren't.	Yes, there is. No, there isn't.
7. How many computers in your house?	There ______ .	There ______ .
8. Are there any brothers or sisters living with you?	Yes, there are. No, there aren't.	Yes, there is. No, there isn't.
9. How many floors in your building?	There ______ .	There ______ .
10. What are you doing now?	He / She ______ .	He / She ______ .
11. What are you doing tonight?	He / She ______ .	He / She ______ .
12. What are you NOT doing now?	He / She ______ .	He / She ______ .
NOW TRY YOUR OWN QUESTIONS		
13.		
14.		
15.		

Exercise 6

Present Continuous: CIRCLE THE ACTION VERBS.
"X" the NON ACTION VERBS.

(Use your phone to translate if you don't know the verb).

HINT ➡  and 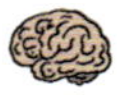 are non-action.

answer ✗	laugh	punch	know
try	make	join	love
help	believe	need	lose
fight	change	open	buy
dislike	go	want	walk

Remember ➡ NON ACTION do NOT get "to be"+ ING.

Exercise 7

Fill in the blanks with "to be" and the (verb) +ING"

1. She ____________________ *(play)* tennis at the moment.
2. Now, he ____________________ *(not do)* anything important.
3. They ____________________ *(come)* to class right now.
4. They ____________________ *(stay)* at home today because it is cold.
5. I ____________________ *(not sleep)* in class right now.
6. We ____________________ *(go)* to Singapore soon.
7. She ____________________ *(not drink)* coffee now.
8. I ____________________ *(work)* hard in this class.
9. You ____________________ *(do)* well.
10. They ____________________ *(not fail)* this class.

UNIT

6 Days, Months and Years

Review Questions:

Write the full sentences. Go back in your book if you need to.

완벽한 문장을 쓰세요. 필요하면 교재를 참조하세요.

- When is your birthday? ______________________________ .
- How many people are there in your family? ______________________ .
- What are you good at? ______________________________ .
- What are your skills? ______________________________ .

Warm-up Questions:

1) What are you not good at?

I am not good at ______________ .
(Activity) ↘ needs "+ing" ➡

2) What can't you do?

I can't ______________ .
(Activity) ↘ NO "ing" ➡

ACTIVITIES:
playing the piano
riding a bicycle
dancing in Hongdae
speaking English
studying for tests
getting up early
playing (basketball / soccer / hockey)

3) What is your favorite day of the week?

My favorite day is ______________
(day)

because ______________ . ➡
(reason)

because...
– I don't have classes on that day
– I get to sleep in
– I meet my boyfriend
– I like the classes on that day
– I usually meet my friends and go to the movies

What is your favorite month of the year?

My favorite month is ______________
(month)

because ______________ . ➡
(reason)

because...
– I like the (summer / winter / spring / fall) months
– my birthday is in this month
– my favorite holiday (Christmas / Children's day, Chuseok) is in this month
– I like the weather in this month

Months:
January February March April May
June July August September October
November December

Dialogue A:

Alex: Hi, Ricardo. Happy New Year!

Ricardo: 1. Can you believe it's December 31st already.

Alex: It's my favorite day of the year. I love the hoping and dreaming and…

Ricardo: And the dancing?

Alex: Yes, I like dancing. 2. It's too bad we have to go to work tomorrow.

Ricardo: It feels strange having New Year's Eve on a Thursday.

Alex: I like it. Thursday is my favorite day of the week.

Ricardo: 3. Why is that?

Alex: My friends and I know a place with cheap chicken wings and sauce only on Thursday. We go almost every week.

Ricardo: But then are you tired on Friday?

Alex: 4. Not too badly. We don't stay out too late. We all have class in the morning. How about you? What is your favorite day of the week?

Ricardo: 5. I am a big fan of Sunday. I know that the next day is Monday, but Sunday is so slow and relaxing. It is the break I need.

Alex: I can understand that.

Substitution Drill: Use the following responses in the above conversation. Practice each with a partner two times. Try to pronounce each word correctly.

		A	B
1.	Can you believe	I can't believe	Seems odd that
2.	It's too bad	It is rough that	The problem is that
3.	Why is that?	Really? Why?	For what reason?
4.	Not too badly.	Not too much.	Only a little bit.
5.	I am a big fan of	I really enjoy	My favorite is

CULTURAL NOTE:

In Western countries, people usually have a 5 day work week:
Monday through Friday. And Sunday is considered the first day of the week.

Comprehension Questions:

What is the date in the dialogue?

____.

What is the day in the dialogue?

____.

Why is Sunday Ricardo's favorite day?

____.

Conversation Concentration

Vocabulary Challenge: Making connections

Months and Holidays: Write the first 3 letters of the month next to the correct holiday.
(You might need to use your dictionary / phone for some of the holidays.)

JANUARY	________	All Fool's Day
FEBRUARY	________	Children's Day
MARCH	________	Christmas
APRIL	________	Chuseok
MAY	________	Constitution Day
JUNE	________	Halloween
JULY	________	Liberation Day
AUGUST	________	Memorial Day
SEPTEMBER	JAN.	New Year's Day
OCTOBER	________	Pepero Day
NOVEMBER	________	Valentine's Day
DECEMBER	________	White Day

Partner A:	*What day is your birthday?*
Partner B:	My birthday is ______________________________ .
Partner B:	What day is your birthday?
Partner A:	My birthday is ______________________________ .

Partner A:	*What is your favorite holiday?*
Partner B:	My favorite holiday is __________________________ . because __________________________________ ____

Partner B:	*What is your favorite holiday?*
Partner A:	My favorite holiday is __________________________ . because __________________________________ ____

SPELLING REVIEW:

Days of the month	Months of the Year	
S _ _ d _ y	J _ _ _ _ _ _	J _ _ _
Mo _ _ a _	F _ _ _ _ _ _ _	A _ _ _ _ _
T _ _ s _ _ _	M _ _ _ _	S _ _ _ _ _ _ _ _
Wed _ _ _ d _ _	A _ _ _ _	O _ _ _ _ _ _
T h _ _ s _ _ _	M _ _	N _ _ _ _ _ _ _
F _ _ _ _ y	J _ _ _	D _ _ _ _ _ _ _
S _ t _ r _ a _		

Conversation Corner: *INTERRUPTING A STRANGER POLITELY*

Please note that "interrupting" is not a rude behavior if done politely and correctly. If not done this way, it can be very rude. You must be careful.

정중하고 정확하게만 한다면 "말을 끊는 것"은 무례한 행동이 아닙니다. 그렇지 못하다면 매우 무례한 경우입니다. 주의해야 합니다.

FIRST: FOLLOW THE FOLLOWING RULES:

1) Have a good reason to interrupt
2) Make eye contact
3) Wait for break in conversation
4) Use polite words

	Interruption	Possible response
More Formal	Pardon the interruption, but… Pardon me, but… I'm sorry to interrupt you, but… I hate to interrupt, but…	No problem. What seems to be the matter? No problem. How can I help?
↕	I don't want to interrupt you, but… I'm sorry, but… Excuse me, but…	It's all right. What can I do for you?
Less Formal	(VERY RUDE ⟶ nothing, just talking)	No. It's all right.

Let's look at the following dialogue:

Woman 1: … and then my son stopped crying and left quietly.

Woman 2: Oh, you are so lucky. Your son is so cute.

Man: Pardon the interruption. I'm in a hurry but I seem to be lost. Would you help me?

Woman 1: No problem. We would love to help. Where are you going?

Man: Witherford Public Library.

Woman 1: Oh … that is just over one block that way.

Man: Excellent. Thank you again.

Get into groups of 3 and practice interrupting.

Interruption 1:	Interruption 2:	Interruption 3:
You need to use the washroom badly. You need to know where the closest washroom is?	You left your cell phone near where two people are sitting. Ask them if they know where your cell phone is.	You don't understand the bus schedule and need help. Interrupt politely and ask which bus goes downtown.

Grammar Focus 1: *Present Continuous Questions*

Pronoun	Affirmative	Negative	Yes/No Question	
I	am (verb)ing *am playing	am not (verb)ing *am not playing	Am I (verb)ing?	Yes, I am. (Yes, you are.) No, I am not. (No, you are not.)
You We They	are (verb)ing *are playing	are not (verb)ing *are not playing *aren't playing	Are you / we / they (verb)ing?	Yes, you are. No, you are not.
He She It	is (verb)ing *is playing	is not (verb)ing *is not playing *isn't playing	Is he / she / it (verb)ing?	Yes, he is. No, he is not.

Making questions in English can get very difficult. However, when the sentence uses the "to be" verb, we move the "to be" verb to the beginning of the sentence as in the following example. (We have already done this in previous chapters.)

영어로 의문문을 만드는 것은 매우 어려울 수 있습니다. 하지만 "be"동사가 사용된 문장일 때 다음의 예에서 보듯이 "be"동사를 문장의 앞으로 옮겨오면 됩니다. (이미 앞 부분에서 다루어 보았던 내용입니다.)

You are going home.

1) find the verb "to be" → You are going home.

2) move the "to be" verb to the front of the sentence. → You are going home.

Are you going home.

*(You → you / are → Are)

3) add "?" to the end of the sentence → Are you going home?

Now you follow the steps in the next example:

They are having fun.

1) find the verb "to be" ➡ ______________________.

2) move the "to be" verb to the front of the sentence. ➡ ______________________.

3) add "?" to the end of the sentence ➡ ______________________.

NOTE 1: Be careful with "I and "you" as they change with question and answer.
* I am running ➡ Am I running? ✔
Are you running? ✔

*(while both are correct, we often don't talk to ourselves in English but to other people, so the second is the better answer)

두 문장 모두 맞는 문장이지만 영어에서는 대화 중에 스스로에게 말을 하는 경우는 없고 타인에게 말하는 것이니 두 번째 문장이 더 좋은 답입니다.

NOTE 2: Remember capital letters (BIG letters). The first word of every sentence has a BIG letter. If you move the "to be" verb there, then it gets a BIG letter, and the word that was there loses its BIG letter.

대문자를 기억하세요. 모든 문장의 첫째 단어는 대문자로 시작합니다. "be" 동사를 문장의 앞으로 옮길 때에는 "be" 동사를 대문자로 시작하고 문장의 앞에 있었던 단어는 대문자로 시작하지 않습니다.

You are dancing. ➡ Are you dancing?

Exercise 1 *Make YES / NO Questions from the sentences below.*

1. They are walking home.
   Are they walking home?
2. He is staying home.
   ____
3. I am dancing.
   ____
4. She is playing computer games.
   ____
5. You are meeting friends.
   ____
6. It is sleeping.
   ____
7. George and Sally are dating.
   ____
8. The birds are eating the seeds.
   ____
9. They are listening to music.
   ____
10. Sarah is watching T.V.
   ____

Grammar Focus 2: *Answering Yes / No questions with the "present continuous".*

"to be" verb:

- Are you tired? → Yes, I am. / No, I'm not.
- Is he tired? → Yes, he is. / No, he is not.
- Am I fat? → Yes, you are / No, you aren't

"to be" verb +ing:

- Are you playing? → Yes, I am. / No, I'm not.
- Is he sleeping? → Yes, he is. / No, he is not.
- Am I dancing? → Yes, you are / No, you aren't

NOTE: Because the answers are the same, it does NOT mean the tense is the same. Remember, "to be" alone is used mostly as an "=" sign, but when used with another verb(+ing), it helps to mean "now".

답이 같다고 해서 시제까지도 같다는 것을 의미하지는 않습니다. "be" 동사만 단독으로 쓰일 때에는 대부분 "그렇다"는 긍정의 의미이지만 다른 동사의 진행형과 함께 사용되면 "현재"라는 의미입니다.

* He is fat. ("is" ➡ "=" He = fat) / He is dancing. ("is" ➡ helper with verb +ing NOW)

Exercise 2 *Answer the following questions with the Yes / No short form.*

1. Are they dancing?
   Yes, they are.
   No, they aren't.
2. Is he helping his mother?
   Yes, ______.
   No, ______.
3. Is she swimming in the lake?
   Yes, ______.
   No, ______.
4. Are we studying hard?
   Yes, ______.
   No, ______.
5. Are you eating potatoes?
   Yes, ______.
   No, ______.
6. Am I going to school today?
   Yes, ______.
   No, ______.
7. Am I writing the answers?
   Yes, ______.
   No, ______.
8. Are you working right now?
   Yes, ______.
   No, ______.

9. Is it sleeping?

Yes, ______________________________ .

No, ______________________________ .

10. Is she meeting her friends?

Yes, ______________________________ .

No, ______________________________ .

Exercise 3 *GROUP WORK:*

Make 5 "Yes / No questions" for other students. Ask them and let them answer. Then let your partners ask their questions to you. Talk to 2 different people.

1. ______________________________ .
2. ______________________________ .
3. ______________________________ .
4. ______________________________ .
5. ______________________________ .

Partner 1 Answers	Partner 2 Answers
1. ____________	1. ____________
2. ____________	2. ____________
3. ____________	3. ____________
4. ____________	4. ____________
5. ____________	5. ____________

Dialogue B:

Ricardo: Hi, Lois!

Lois: Hi boys. 1. Have you picked your New Year's Resolution?

Ricardo: I want to 2. start exercising again.

Alex: I thought you wanted to improve your grades?

Ricardo: 3. That, too.

Lois: You told me you wanted to make more money.

Ricardo: I would like to be skinny, smart, and rich next year.

Alex: Good luck.

Ricardo: At least I have a resolution!

Alex: 4. I can't think of one.

Lois: What are you not good at?

Alex: Many things.

Lois: What can't you do?

Alex: I can't fly.

Ricardo: You can't quit smoking!

Lois: That's a good one!

Alex: OK. OK. I'll try to quit smoking. But let me have just one more!

Ricardo: Come on! 5. You can do this!

Popular New Year's Resolutions:
*Get good grades *Earn more money
*Travel *Help others or volunteer
*Quit smoking *Lose weight

Substitution Drill: Use the following responses in the above conversation. Practice each with a partner two times. Try to pronounce each word correctly.

		A	B
1.	Have you picked your	Did you choose any	What are your
2.	start exercising again.	hit the gym.	get into shape.
3.	That, too.	Sure. I would like that as well.	And that!
4.	I can't think of one.	I can't think of anything.	I am drawing a blank.
5.	You can do this!	Be strong.	I believe in you.

CULTURAL NOTE:

Many people make a New Year's Resolution.
This is a promise to make a positive change for next year.

Conversation Corner: *Interrupting a friend / person you know*

Interrupting a friend or someone you know to ask a question is easier. With a friend, we can be less formal. With a co-worker, or professor, we still should be formal. Remember, in a class, the best way to politely interrupt is to raise your hand and wait to be called on.

질문을 하기 위해 친구나 지인의 말을 끊는 것은 쉽습니다. 친구와의 사이에서는 좀 더 자유로울 수 있습니다. 동료나 교수님에게는 좀 예의를 갖추어야 합니다. 강의실에서 정중하게 말을 끊는 방법은 손을 든 뒤 호명될 때까지 기다리는 것입니다.

Let's review:

Who should we talk "MORE FORMAL" to?	Who should we talk "LESS FORMAL" to? (CASUAL)

Important words to study for interrupting a friend (LESS FORMAL)

친구의 말을 끊을 때 사용할 수 있는 중요한 표현들. (자유로운 표현)

- Let me stop you there for a second. I think that...
- Hold on. Are you saying that...
- Let me interject here and say...
- Can I just say that...
- Wait a second. I should say that...
- Sorry, but I think...
- Is it okay if I jump in for a second?
- Can I throw my two cents in?

Important words for interrupting a person you know (MORE FORMAL)

지인의 말을 끊을 때 사용할 수 있는 중요한 표현들.(격식을 갖춘 표현)

- Could I stop you there for a second and just quickly say that...
- Sorry, but could I just mention that...
- Pardon the interruption but I need to say...
- I'm sorry to interrupt but it needs to be said that...
- I hate to stop you but could I just add that...
- If I might add something...

Practice the above with a partner, then practice the situations below.

"What is your favorite day of the week?" Let them answer and try to politely interrupt to add something. "일주일 중 어느 요일을 가장 좋아해?" 상대가 대답할 때 정중히 말을 끊고 첨언해 보세요.	Start talking about your favorite music and let your partner interrupt you. 당신이 가장 좋아하는 음악에 대해 말을 하고 상대방이 당신의 말을 끊도록 해 보세요.	Pretend your partner is your grandfather telling a long boring story. Interrupt him politely. 상대방이 길고 지루한 얘기를 늘어놓는 할아버지라고 가정하세요. 정중하게 말을 끊어보세요.

Present Continuous and "WWWWW and H":

As in Unit 4,WWWWW and H" (question words), are placed at the beginning of the sentence followed by the verb "to be", subject, then "verb"+ing.

4과에서와 마찬가지로 의문사는 문장의 앞에 놓이고 그 뒤에 "be"동사가 따라오며 그 다음에 주어와 "동사원형" +ing가 따라옵니다.

Ex. What are you doing? / Where are you going?
When are you leaving? / Who is making that noise?
Why are you eating so fast? / How are they studying for the exam?

Exercise 4 *In the following exercise, use the answer to make the question. Replace the underlined word with a "WWWWW and H" question word. The first one is done for you.*

1. When is she coming here?
   She is coming here at 10 o'clock.

2. Why ______________________ ?
   He is exercising because he wants to lose weight.

3. ______________________ ?
   They are going to the movie theater.

4. ______________________ ?
   My boss is yelling again.

5. ______________________ ?
   She is looking for her pencil.

6. ______________________ ?
   It is wearing a small coat.

7. ______________________ ?
   I am studying in the classroom right now.

8. ______________________ ?
   I am studying in the classroom right now.

9. ______________________________________ ?

The group "Small Bang" is playing at the club.

10. ______________________________________ ?

The party is starting at 7 p.m.

11. ______________________________________ ?

We are going to the beach because we want to swim.

12. ______________________________________ ?

We are going to the beach by bus.

Exercise 5 *Now make answers for the questions with the answers in the parentheses (   ).*

1. Where is he going? (home)

He is going home.

2. When is she coming ? (7 p.m.)

____

3. Why are you sleeping? (because I am tired)

____

4. How is she dealing with her stress? (with yoga)

____

5. What are they buying? (a new shirt)

____

6. Why are we making so much kimbab? (for the picnic)

____

7. Who is coming to the party? (everybody)

____

8. When am I playing tennis? (next Saturday)

____

9. How are you losing weight? (because I am on a diet)

____

10. Where is everyone going tonight? (to the club)

____

11. What am I writing? (answers to the questions)

____

12. Who is working at the restaurant now? (Sherry)

____

Exercise 6

PICTURE Write the correct form of the Present Continuous for the following pictures.

**USE THE HINT VOCABULARY*

	HINT: Where... ? ...at home.	? .
	What... ? ...a cake.	? .
	Why... ? ...to keep his teeth white.	? .
	Where... ? ...at the restaurant.	? .
	What... ? ...a guitar.	? .
	Why...(smiling)? ...because he likes soccer.	? .

TOEIC VOCABULARY

Read the following common TOEIC words. Memorize so that you can do well on the TOEIC. Write the Korean and English below in the blanks two times to help you learn.

rise: 오르다. 일어나다.
Prices have risen recently because of high oil prices.
(최근 유가가 올라서 물가가 올랐다.)

________ /________ ________ /________

review: 복습(하다).
In English study, review is a must.
(영어 학습에서 복습은 필수이다.)

________ /________ ________ /________

recover: 회복하다.
Father easily recovered from the illness.
(아버지는 질병에서 쉽게 회복하셨다.)

________ /________ ________ /________

admit: 인정하다.
He admitted that he had stolen the gem.
(그는 보석을 훔쳤다는 것을 인정했다.)

________ /________ ________ /________

put off: 연기하다.
Never put off till tomorrow what you should do today.
(오늘 해야 할 일을 절대 내일로 미루지 마라.)

________ /________ ________ /________

the thing: 중요한 것.
The thing is that it should be done right now.
(중요한 것은 그 일을 지금 당장 해야 한다는 것이다.)

________ /________ ________ /________

something: 어떤 것, 중요한 것.
Would you give me something to eat?
(먹을 것 좀 주시겠습니까?)

________ /________ ________ /________

angry: 화가 난.
She was very angry about his being lazy.
(그녀는 그가 게을러서 매우 화가 났다.)

________ /________ ________ /________

give up: 포기하다.
He never gives up whatever the case.
(그는 어떤 경우라도 절대 포기하지 않는다.)

________ /________ ________ /________

help: 돕다.
Heaven helps those who help themselves.
(하늘은 스스로 돕는 자를 돕는다.)

________ /________ ________ /________

read: 읽다.
I have read this book more than 10 times.
(이 책을 10번 이상 읽었다.)

________ /________ ________ /________

expensive: 비싼.
What is expensive is not always a good thing.
(비싼 것이 항상 좋은 것만은 아니다.)

________ /________ ________ /________

have: 가지고 있다.
This money is all that I have with me.
(이 돈이 내가 가지고 있는 돈 전부입니다.)

________ /________ ________ /________

explain: 설명하다.
The ability to explain in easy words is important.
(쉬운 말로 설명할 수 있는 능력이 중요하다.)

________ /________ ________ /________

habit: 습관.
Bad habits die hard.
(악습은 쉽게 사라지지 않는다.)

________ /________ ________ /________

present: 선물, 현재의, 주다.
As many children as came were given some presents.
(온 어린이들에게는 선물이 주어졌다.)

________ /________ ________ /________

rule: 규칙.
Every rule has some exceptions.
(모든 규칙은 약간의 예외가 있다.)

__________ /__________ __________ /__________

maintain: 유지하다, 관리하다, 주장하다.
The equipment should be maintained thoroughly.
(장비는 철저하게 관리되어야 한다.)

__________ /__________ __________ /__________

decide: 결정하다.
She decided to separate from him.
(그녀는 그와 헤어지기로 결심했다.)

__________ /__________ __________ /__________

study: 공부하다.
While he was studying, somebody rang the bell.
(그가 공부하는 중에 누군가가 초인종을 눌렀다.)

__________ /__________ __________ /__________

grow: 성장하다.
As he grew old, he became more and more talkative.
(나이가 들어감에 따라 그는 점점 더 수다스러워졌다.)

__________ /__________ __________ /__________

company: 회사.
He got a job at a company just after graduation.
(그는 졸업 직후 회사에 취업했다.)

__________ /__________ __________ /__________

accident: 사고.
On the way to school, I witnessed an accident.
(학교 오는 길에 사고를 목격했다.)

__________ /__________ __________ /__________

live: 살다.
This is the house where I live.
(여기가 제가 살고 있는 집입니다.)

__________ /__________ __________ /__________

succeed: 성공하다.
This is the way I succeeded in my English study.
(이것이 내가 영어 학습에서 성공항 방법이다.)

__________ /__________ __________ /__________

sincere: 진실한.
Being sincere is the most important factor.
(진실한 것이 가장 중요한 요소이다.)

__________ /__________ __________ /__________

cover: 뒤덮다.
Mt. Halla may be covered with snow by now.
(한라산은 지금쯤 눈으로 뒤덮여 있을 것이다.)

__________ /__________ __________ /__________

praise: 칭찬(하다.)
Praise makes an elephant dance.
(칭찬은 코끼리도 춤추게 한다.)

__________ /__________ __________ /__________

export: 수출하다.
Korea exports several kinds of mobile phones.
(한국은 다양한 종류의 이동전화를 수출한다.)

__________ /__________ __________ /__________

criminal: 범인.
The criminal is still at large.
(범인은 아직도 도피 중이다.)

__________ /__________ __________ /__________

UNIT

7 Habits and Daily Routines

Review Questions:

- What is your favorite month of the year? ______________________________ .
- What is your hobby? ______________________________ .
- Where do you live? ______________________________ .
- What does your mother do? ______________________________ .
- What are you not good at? ______________________________ .

Warm-up Questions:

- What is your favorite food?

  I like to eat ______________ .
  (name of food in English)

- What is your favorite drink?

  I like to drink ______________ .

- What kind of movies do you like?

  I like to watch ______________ .

- What is your favorite sport to watch?

  I like to watch ______________ .

- What is your favorite sport?

  I like to play ______________ .

Popular Sports:
Soccer, Cricket, Basketball, Hockey, Tennis, Volleyball, Baseball, Golf, Football, Table Tennis (Ping Pong)

Korean Dishes in English:

김치:	Kimchi: fermented cabbage with granulated pepper and a variety of liquid salted fishes
김밥:	Kimbab: rice and assorted vegetables rolled in seaweed laver
된장:	Dwenjang: fermented soy bean
××볶음:	XX pokkum: stir-fried XX
갈비:	Kalbi: Traditional Korean self-cooking BBQ meats with side dishes
떡볶이:	Ddokpokki: Rice cakes cooked in a hot red pepper sauce.

Types of meat:
Beef (cow), chicken, fish, mutton (sheep), and pork (pig).

Types of drinks:
Beer, coffee, juice, milk, soda, tea, and water.

Popular genres of movies:
Action, Adventure. Comedy, Crime, Drama, Horror, Romance, Thriller, Science Fiction

Dialogue A:

Akari: Hey Alex! 1. Wait for me,
I will walk to the cafeteria with you.

Alex: Hi Akari. I didn't expect to see you on campus. I thought you only studied on Monday, Wednesday and Friday.

Akari: True! I decided to go to the gym on my days off. I just finished my workout. I am starving.
2. Can I tag along?

Alex: Sure! I am planning on having some kimchi tsigae. It is my favorite dish.
I love eating at the cafeteria on Thursdays.

Akari: I am 3. not a fan of tsigae. I prefer it as side dish.
I will order some kimbab. What are your plans after classes?

Alex: I am working on a few projects.

Akari: I want to go 4. check out a flick at CGV. There are some great movies showing there at the moment. Do you want to go see a movie?

Alex: 5. I will take a raincheck. I have lots of work to get done. I hate doing homework on the weekend. How about going to see that new horror movie on Saturday?

Akari: That would be great! Hopefully, the line up at the box office is not as long as the cafeteria!

Alex: If the line at the CGV is this long, we'll go somewhere else!

Substitution Drill: Use the following responses in the above conversation. Practice each with a partner two times. Try to pronounce each word correctly.

		A	B
1.	Wait for me,	Hold on,	Wait up,
2.	Can I tag along?	Can I join you?	Can we go together?
3.	not a fan of	dislike	not impressed by
4.	check out a flick	watch a movie	see a film
5.	I will take a raincheck.	I want to but not today.	Another time later is better.

CULTURAL NOTE:

"RAINCHECK": This is a very polite way of accepting an offer, but for a better time. In the past, it was used in case of rain, but now it is used regardless of the weather!

Conversation Corner 1:

Explaining why you can't stay / talk longer. (polite / impolite)

What do you say when you are talking to someone but you need to leave? How do you politely end the conversation? Here are some "Exit" sentences to study.

대화 중 자리를 떠야 할 때 상대방에게 어떻게 말하십니까? 어떻게 하면 정중하게 대화를 끝낼 수 있을까요? 대화를 끝내기 위해 알아둘 표현이 다음에 있습니다.

- I'm sorry but I have to go. I... (죄송하지만 가봐야겠네요.)
- I hate to leave so quickly but I... (이렇게 빨리 가기는 싫지만…)
- I hate to ask but can we talk later? I... (무리한 요구 같지만 나중에 다시 대화할 수 있을까요?)
- Please don't think I'm rude but I... (무례하다고 생각하지는 마세요…)
- I hate to do this to you but I... (이렇게 하기는 싫지만…)
- Sorry but I should get going. I... (죄송하지만 가봐야겠는데요…)

Must... Have to... Should... Need to...

Must / Have to- would imply that you are obligated to leave.
It tells others that you cannot stay.

Must와 Have to는 가야 할 의무가 있다는 것을 내포한다. 더 이상 체류할 수 없다는 것을 상대방에게 말한다.

Should / need to- implies that you could stay, but would prefer to go.

Should와 need to는 머무를 수 있지만 가고 싶다는 의미를 내포한다.

THREE MORE REASONS: What do you say to friends when you have to go? Make three more reasons using "Must" and "Should". After you complete your writing find a classmate that has the same or similar sentences as you.

이유 세 개 더: 가야 할 때 친구에게 뭐라고 말하십니까? "must"와 "should"를 사용하여 세 개의 이유를 더 만들어 보세요. 작문을 다한 뒤 당신과 동일하거나 비슷한 문장을 쓴 친구가 있는가 찾아보세요.

I must...	I should...

Grammar Focus 1: *Present Simple*

This is used to describe actions in the present that are habit (습관, 습성) *or routine* (일과, 판에 박힌)

This is used with frequency especially with the question "How often...?". Words associated with the present simple tense are:

현재 시제는 "얼마나 자주?"라는 빈도를 묻는 질문과 함께 사용된다. 현재시제와 관련된 단어는 다음과 같다:

A) always, usually, often, sometimes, occasionally, rarely, never
B) once a... twice a... three times a... four times a... five times a...
C) Mondays, Tuesdays, Wednesdays, mornings, evenings, afternoons
D) daily, weekly, monthly, yearly, hourly

Ex. I eat breakfast in the mornings. He eats dinner at a restaurant twice a month.

Pronoun	Affirmative	Negative(not)	Inquisitive?(Question)	
I You We They	play	don't play	Do I play... ?	Yes, I do. / No, I don't.
	go	don't go	Do you go... ?	Yes, you do. / No, you don't.
	eat	don't eat	Do we eat... ?	Yes, we do. / No, we don't.
	study	don't study	Do they study... ?	Yes they do. / No, they don't.
	do	don't do	Do I do... ?	Yes, I do. / No, I don't.
	drink	don't drink	Do you drink... ?	Yes, you do. / No, you don't.

He She It (+S)	plays goes eats studies does drinks	doesn't play doesn't go doesn't eat doesn't study doesn't do doesn't drink	Does he play… ? Does she go… ? Does it eat… ? Does he study… ? Does she do… ? Does it drink… ?	Yes, he does. / No, he doesn't. Yes, she does. / No, she doesn't. Yes, it does. / No, it doesn't. Yes, he does. / No, he doesn't. Yes, she does. / No, she doesn't. Yes, it does. / No, it doesn't.

LOOK at the chart above very carefully. (위의 표를 잘 보세요.)
You should see 4 important things. (네 가지 중요한 사항을 알아야 합니다.)

1) There is NO "to be" verb. ("be"동사가 없습니다.)
2) There is NO "+ ing". ("동사원형 +ing" 형태가 없습니다.)
3) NOT → don't / doesn't Do / Does… ? (부정문으로 묻지 않고 긍정문으로 묻습니다.)
4) HE SHE IT are special. In English, HE SHE IT have an "S" as well.
3인칭 단수인 He, She, It은 특별합니다. 영어에서 3인칭 단수가 주어이고 동사 시제가 현재일 때에는 동사원형 뒤에 "(e)s"를 붙입니다.

Exercise 1 *Fill in the blanks with the correct form of the verb.*

1. I eat cookies. He ______________________ cookies.
2. You play soccer. She ______________________ soccer.
3. They sleep at night. It ______________________ at night.
4. We see a movie. He ______________________ a movie.
5. I dance every Saturday. She ______________________ every Saturday.
6. You walk in the park. It ______________________ in the park.

Exercise 2 *Fill in the blanks with the correct form of the verbs below.*

Fill in the blanks with the correct form of the verb "to walk".	*Fill in the blanks with the correct form of the verb "to go".*
1. I ___walk___ to university every day.	6. I ___go___ to university every day.
2. You ________ to work every day.	7. You ________ to work every day.
3. He ________ to the park every day.	8. He ________ to the park every day.
4. They ________ to school every day.	9. They ________ to school every day.
5. She ________ home every day.	10. She ________ home every day.

Exceptions:
will, can, may, could, shall, might, would, should, ought to
NO "HE / SHE / IT S"

Exercise 3 *Write the sentences with the correct form of the verb:*

1. (he/go to school every day)

   He goes to school every day.

2. (I/like swimming)

3. (you/play badminton on Saturdays)

4. (the class/begin at 9 a.m.)

5. (they/sometimes go to the cinema)

6. (she/love chocolate)

7. (they/live in London)

8. (he/may work in a restaurant)

9. (Lucy/can play the guitar)

10. (we/cook every day)

11. (he/clean the house at the weekends)

12. (I/like reading detective stories)

Dialogue B:

Alex: 1. What did you think of the movie?

Akari: Actually, it didn't scare me. I have seen better horror movies 2. in the past. However, I liked the popcorn.

Alex: I was not too impressed by it either. I like movies that have a good story not just blood and guts. It was a bit too gory.

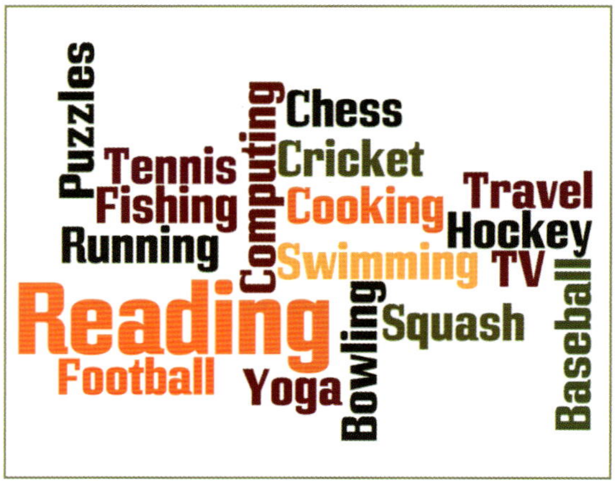

Akari: 3. How about getting a coffee?

Alex: That would be perfect! Let's find a place where we can sit outside. It is not too chilly out and tonight there is a full moon.

Akari: As long as there are no werewolves and you don't start talking about astronomy. 4. That was my worst subject last year.

Alex: Well, if you don't talk about art history, 5. then it is a deal! I failed that course last semester. Lunch has always been my best subject.

Akari: (laughing). Me too. Maybe we should get a bite with that coffee too. You remind me how hungry I am.

Alex: I know a nice little café with homemade bread and sandwiches. Let's go this way. It is just up here on the left.

Substitution Drill: Use the following responses in the above conversation. Practice each with a partner two times. Try to pronounce each word correctly.

		A	B
1.	What did you think of the movie?	Did you like the movie?	Any thoughts on the movie?
2.	in the past	before now	sometime ago
3.	How about getting a coffee?	Should we get a coffee?	What about a nice cup of coffee now?
4.	That was my worst subject	That is the subject where I struggled the most	I did terribly in that subject
5.	then it is a deal!	then we have an agreement!	then we are in agreement!

Conversation Corner 2: *Asking a person to move out of the way. (polite / impolite)*

Crowded streets during parade

*Hey...**

Excuse me...

Pardon me...

Please move out of my way...

Excuse me. Sorry, pardon me!

*Get out of my way!**

Sorry, buy can I get past you?

*Do you mind?**

May I get by you?

*Hurry up!**

**can be rude... be careful using these!!*

Please: (used as a polite addition to requests,commands, etc.)

Please: 정중하게 요청하거나 지시할 때 사용합니다.

Thank You: expressing one's gratitude or thanks

Thank you: 감사함을 표현할 때 사용합니다.

May I... : When you use "May I..." it is a very polite form of speech.
One should always say "please" and "thank you," but if you begin a sentence with "May I..." then usually you do not have to say "please."

"May I ..."는 매우 정중한 어법입니다. "please"와 "thank you"를 항상 사용하는 것이 좋지만 "May I ..."로 문장을 시작할 때에는 "please"를 사용할 필요는 없습니다.

AFTER HEARING "EXCUSE ME" or any of the above.

Excuse me...

Oh sorry. Here you are.

My bad. Go ahead!

Sorry. (motion with hand)

Sure. Go on past.

PRACTICE: Walk around the room. Practice the following. As well, if you find yourself moving the same way, remember that most people go "left".

Grammar Focus 2: *Verb Conjugation and Spelling*

HE / SHE / IT ➡ ES

- Rule: If the last letter of the verb ends in "ch, sh, s, o, x, z", then you add an "es"

He	ch	catches	marches	watches		
	sh	pushes	washes	wishes	rushes	
She	s	kisses	misses	passes		
	o	does	goes	echoes		
It	x	boxes	coaxes	relaxes	fixes	mixes
	z	buzzes	dozes			

HE / SHE / IT –YS vs. IES

- Rule: If the letter before the "y" is a vowel, you add "s".

_ y ys EX. play : plays / obey: obeys

↑

(a, e, i, o ,u)

If the letter before the "y" is not a vowel (a consonant), then the "y" changes to "i" and you add "es".

_ y ~~y~~ ies EX. study: studies / try : tries

↑

~~(a, e, i, o, u)~~

Exercise 1 *SPELLING PRACTICE*

box: ______	pass: ______	enjoy: ______
watch: ______	do: ______	relax: ______
play: ______	obey: ______	punch: ______
run: ______	study: ______	miss: ______
stay: ______	eat: ______	walk: ______
try: ______	cook: ______	echo: ______
cry: ______	marry: ______	dry: ______
fix: ______	go: ______	pray: ______

Exercise 2 Fill in the blanks with the correct form of the verb.

1. We always __________ *(walk)* home from school.
2. She never __________ *(drink)* diet sodas.
3. You __________ *(can)* go next.
4. I __________ *(play)* tennis every Saturday.
5. He __________ *(dance)* very well.
6. My neighbor __________ *(work)* at the hospital.
7. He __________ *(eat)* fish.
8. The student always __________ *(study)* for their tests.
9. She __________ *(live)* in California.
10. The store usually __________ *(close)* at 10 p.m.
11. She __________ *(watch)* the T.V.
12. He __________ *(talk)* quietly in class.
13. Curtis __________ *(eat)* breakfast in the morning.
14. You __________ *(like)* playing computer.
15. He __________ *(march)*.

Exercise 3 Write full sentences for the following:

1. (we/often watch T.V.)

____

2. (I/hate mushrooms)

____

3. (she/visit her grandmother every Christmas)

____

4. (they/use the Internet every evening)

____

5. (you/often go swimming)

____

6. (John/hate waiting for the bus)

____

7. (Lucy and Jill/want to go out tonight)

____

8. (I/usually stay at home on Fridays)

____

9. (he/love driving fast cars)

____

10. (they/often have parties)

____

Exercise 4 *DAILY ROUTINES. Write your daily routine for MONDAY and SATURDAY. USE THE VERBS PROVIDED. You do NOT have to use them all. Choose 8 and write sentences.*

study, eat, lunch, wake up, eat dinner, go to work, eat breakfast, take a shower, put on clothes, drink coffee, play phone games, exercise, go to sleep, watch T.V., surf the Internet, go shopping

Ex. On Monday, I wake up at 8:00 a.m.
On Saturday, I wake up at 11:30 a.m.

MONDAY	SATURDAY
1. ____________	1. ____________
2. ____________	2. ____________
3. ____________	3. ____________
4. ____________	4. ____________
5. ____________	5. ____________
6. ____________	6. ____________

Now find a partner and write down his / her schedule using HE / SHE / IT → S!

PARTNER: ______________________________

MONDAY	SATURDAY
1. ____________________	1. ____________________
2. ____________________	2. ____________________
3. ____________________	3. ____________________
4. ____________________	4. ____________________
5. ____________________	5. ____________________
6. ____________________	6. ____________________

TOEIC VOCABULARY

Read the following common TOEIC words. Memorize so that you can do well on the TOEIC. Write the Korean and English below in the blanks two times to help you learn.

satisfy: 만족시키다.
Many Asians are satisfied with Korean pop music.
(많은 아시아인들이 한국의 대중음악에 만족한다.)

________ /________ ________ /________

allow: 허용하다.
People are not allowed to park here.
(이 곳에 주차할 수 없습니다.)

________ /________ ________ /________

speak: 말하다.
English is spoken all over the world.
(영어는 세계 곳곳에서 사용되고 있다.)

________ /________ ________ /________

suppose: 가정하다.
They are supposed to meet here at noon.
(그들은 정오에 이곳에서 만나기로 되어 있다.)

________ /________ ________ /________

shock: 놀라게 하다.
She was shocked to hear that her mother had been dead.
(그녀는 어머님이 돌아가셨다는 소식을 듣고 충격을 받았다.)

________ /________ ________ /________

pay: 지불하다.
Education pays.
(교육은 받은 만큼의 대가를 지불한다.)

________ /________ ________ /________

explain: 설명하다.
Could you explain to me of the meaning of this word?
(이 단어의 의미를 제게 설명해 주시겠습니까?)

________ /________ ________ /________

say: 말하다.
What they said cannot be true.
(사람들이 한 말이 사실일 리가 없다.)

________ /________ ________ /________

afford: 여유를 가지고 있다.
I cannot afford to buy a new car for the moment.
(지금으로서는 새 차를 살 여유가 없다.)

________ /________ ________ /________

drop: 들르다.
May I drop by on the way to the station?
(역으로 가는 길에 잠깐 들러도 될까요?)

________ /________ ________ /________

respond: 반응하다.
You may well respond to them like that.
(그들에게 그렇게 반응하는 것이 당연하다.)

________ /________ ________ /________

obey: 복종하다.
We must obey our parents whatever the case.
(어떤 경우라도 부모님께 복종해야 한다.)

________ /________ ________ /________

believe: 믿다.
You must be a fool to believe what he said.
(그가 한 말을 믿다니 당신은 바보로구만.)

________ /________ ________ /________

meet: 만나다.
You must not meet her any more.
(그 여자를 만나지 않아야 한다.)

________ /________ ________ /________

die: 죽다.
All of us will die in due time.
(우리 모두는 때가 되면 죽는다.)

________ /________ ________ /________

hard: 열심히.
You should have studied harder when young.
(어렸을 때 좀 더 열심히 공부를 했었어야지.)

________ /________ ________ /________

party: 파티.
I should not have gone to the party last night.
(어젯밤 파티에 가지 않았어야 했는데.)

____ /____ ____ /____

necessary: 필요한.
It is necessary that he (should) go at once.
(그 사람이 즉시 가는 것이 필요해.)

____ /____ ____ /____

marry: 결혼하다.
They recommended that I should marry her.
(사람들은 내게 그녀와 결혼하라고 추천했다.)

____ /____ ____ /____

would: ~하기를 원하다.
I would (do it) if I could (do it).
(할 수만 있다면 할 텐데.)

____ /____ ____ /____

swim: 수영하다.
We would go swimming on a fine day.
(날씨가 좋은 날이면 수영을 하러 가곤 했었다.)

____ /____ ____ /____

open: 열리다.
The door would not open.
(문이 열릴 생각을 하지 않았다.)

____ /____ ____ /____

care: 좋아하다.
Would you care for another helping?
(밥 한 공기 더 드시겠습니까?)

____ /____ ____ /____

follow: 따르다.
You ought to follow their instruction.
(그들의 지시를 따라야 한다.)

____ /____ ____ /____

catch: 잡다.
If you run after two hares, you will catch neither.
(두 마리 토끼를 좇으면 한 마리도 못 잡을 것이다.)

____ /____ ____ /____

change: 바꾸다.
If it should rain tonight, I will change my name.
(오늘 밤 비가 온다면 내 이름을 바꾸겠다.)

____ /____ ____ /____

accept: 받아들이다.
If I were you, I would accept that proposal.
(내가 너라면 그 제안을 받아들일 텐데.)

____ /____ ____ /____

come: 오다.
What if she shouldn't come?
(그녀가 오지 않으면 어쩌지?)

____ /____ ____ /____

difficult: 어려운:
Success in life is a difficult thing to achieve.
(삶에서의 성공은 성취하기 어려운 것이다.)

____ /____ ____ /____

discuss: 토론하다.
At last, they decided to discuss the matter in detail.
(마침내 그들은 그 문제를 심도있게 토론하기로 했다.)

____ /____ ____ /____

TOEIC GRAMMAR EXERCISES:

Choose the correct answer. Some of the grammar has advanced rules. We are hoping that by exposure, we can expand on your knowledge base.

1) There _____ many soccer players that _____ coming from another country.
   A) am / are B) is / is
   C) are /are D) aren't / am not

2) Every morning, he _____ up at 6 am.
   A) get B) getting
   C) gets D) is get

3) We _____ a new program on your computers that will help send bills to clients easier.
   A) is installing B) are installing
   C) installs D) install

4) My favorite band _____ tonight in the park. I can't wait!
   A) plays B) play
   C) is playing D) are playing

5) Look out! The ball _____ at you.
   A) is coming B) are coming
   C) comes D) come

6) He _____ coming tonight. He called and said he can't make it.
   A) doesn't B) aren't
   C) don't D) isn't

7) _____ you really _____ to lie to me? You are bad at it.
   A) Do / try B) Does / tries
   C) Is / trying D) Are / trying

8) He _____ new candidates this morning. Please call back later.
   A) is interviewing B) are interview
   C) does interview D) interviewing

9) He _____ playing soccer in his free time.
   A) enjoys B) enjoies
   C) enjoyes D) enjoy

10) Bill always _____ to music before he goes to sleep.
   A) is hearing B) hears
   C) Is listening D) listens

11) I admire Bob. He _____ every morning before I even wake up.
   A) is exercising B) is exerciseing
   C) exercises D) do exercises

12) I usually _____ up at 6:30 a.m., but I _____ up now at 8:30 a.m. because it is a holiday.
   A) am waking / am waking B) am waking / wake
   C) wake / am waking D) wake / wake

13) I'm sorry. They _____ at the moment. They usually _____ new customers at 10:30 a.m.
   A) are working / are seeing B) are working / see
   C) work / see D) work / are seeing

14) He _____ the new color of the walls. He wants to repaint.
   A) isn't liking B) don't like
   C) doesn't liking D) doesn't like

15) She _____ very skilled in the kitchen. She _____ cook all sorts of delicious meals.
   A) is / can B) is being / cans
   C) is / cans D) are / cans

UNIT

8 We Always Go to Busan in the Summer

Review Questions:

- What is your favorite kind of movie? My favorite kind of movie is ________________ .
  sport to watch? ________________ .
  drink? ________________ .
  food? ________________ .
- What kinds of things are you not good at? ________________ .
- What do you want to be in the future? ________________ .

Warm-up Questions:

22) Where have you travelled?

I have travelled to ________________ .

(city in Korea/city and country out of Korea)

23) Where would you like to travel?

(Where do you want to go?)

I would like to travel to ________________ .

(city in Korea/city and country out of Korea)

24) Think of 3 good things and 3 bad things about travelling. Three good things about travelling are ________________ , ________________ , and ________________ .

(good reasons about travelling)

Three bad things about travelling are ________________ , ________________ , and ________________ .

(bad reasons about travelling)

In Korea, the city name only is ok.
"I have travelled to Busan."

Out of Korea,
you can say country only,
or city and country.
"I have travelled to Tokyo, Japan".

Good Things
- I get to see new places.
- I get to relax.
- I get to enjoy beaches and outdoors.
- ________________

Bad Things
- I spend too much money.
- I find riding on buses and cars long and boring.
- I often eat too much junk food.
- ________________

TASK: How good is your geography?

With a partner, look at these Korean city names. Can you write them in English?
(NOTE: Cities in Korea all end with 시, which means 'city'. We don't usually do this in English.)
So, take turns to ask your partner questions about spelling.

상대방과 함께 다음의 한국도시명을 보세요. 영어로 쓸 수 있겠습니까?
주의사항: 한국어로 도시는 "시"로 끝나고 "city"를 의미하지만 영어에서는 별도로 표기하지 않습니다.

Ex. A: How do you spell 서울 in English?
B: It's S-E-O-U-L.

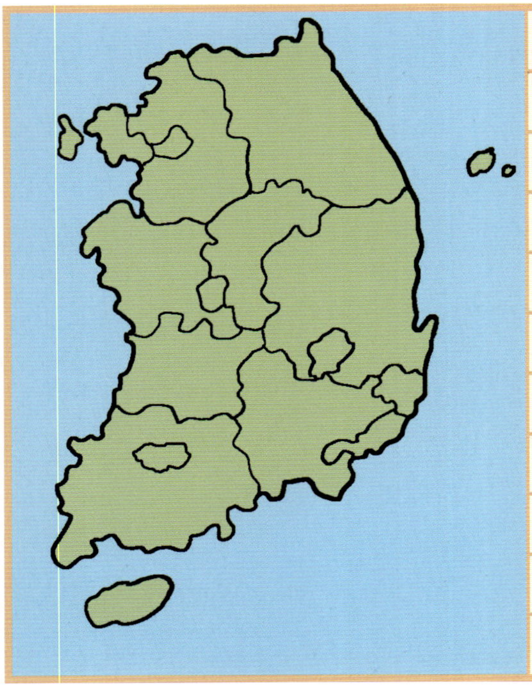

Korean	**English**
EX. 서울특별시	EX. Seoul
1. 보령시	
2. 춘천시	
3. 안동시	
4. 포천시	
5. 의정부시	
6. 부산광역시	
7. 목포시	
8. 인천광역시	
9. 광주광역시	

Write the number of each city where you think it is in Korea.

Ex. *Bo-geun:* *"Hey Min-su, where do you think Seoul is on this map?"*
Min-su: *"Hm, I think it's here".*
I don't know, maybe here?
I have no idea!

Once you have labelled the map, check a detailed map on your phone to see how accurate you were.

Dialogue A:

John: Wow. 1. I really enjoyed spending time with you tonight. You are a lot of fun to hang out with.

Sofia: I had a great time too. I enjoy drinking coffee and talking. As well, you are very easy to talk to. I hope I didn't talk about Italy too much. I sometimes 2. miss being there.

John: No, not at all. It was very interesting and I enjoy listening to you. I love travelling, and now I have another place that I need to visit.

Sofia: I love travelling too, especially to sunny places.

John: I would love to go to the beaches more often but travelling can get expensive. Thailand and Indonesia have great beaches but the hotels can 3. get pricy.

Sofia: You don't need to leave Korea. Korea has beautiful beaches, too.

John: You mean Haeundae? No, thanks. 4. There are too many people.

Sofia: I agree. I recommend Gyeongpodae in Gangneung. It is quiet, clean and not too far. My friends and I go there every summer.

John: I haven't been there yet. Hmm. Maybe I 5. should look into it!

Sofia: Perhaps you can join my friends and me later next month.

John: Wow! Sounds great!

Substitution Drill: Use the following responses in the above conversation. Practice each with a partner two times. Try to pronounce each word correctly.

		A	B
1.	I really enjoyed spending time	I had a lot of fun	I had a good time
2.	miss being there.	wish I were still there.	want to see my own country again.
3.	get pricy.	be expensive.	cost too much.
4.	There are too many people.	It is too crowded.	There are so many people it is no fun.
5.	should look into it!	research it more.	try to find more information about it.

Comprehension Questions:

no "es"→
no "s" in answer

1. What does Sofia miss?

   Sofia misses ______________________.

2. What do they love doing?

   They love ______________________.

3. What beach does Sofia recommend?

   ______________________.

4. Who goes to Gyeongpodae every summer?

   ______________________.

5. What does Sofia enjoy?

   ______________________.

6. What does John enjoy?

   ______________________.

Conversation Corner: *AGREEING with another person* (타인에게 동의하기)

There are a lot of great ways to agree to an opinion. Look at the following and practice with a partner. (의견에 동의하는 방법은 매우 많습니다. 다음 표현을 보고 상대방과 연습하세요.)

	Not Formal (허물없는 표현) (for friends)	**Formal** (예의를 갖춘 표현) (for elders / important people)
weakly agree → strongly agree	• Great idea! • Definitely! • I couldn't agree with you more. • That's for sure. • That's exactly how I feel. • I guess so. • Could be. • If you think so.	• You're absolutely right. • I agree with you 100 percent. • Absolutely. • That's so true. • I would agree with some of what you say. • I suppose so. • Hmm. I'll have to think about that.

BUT… what if you DON'T AGREE?: Expressing Disagreement (그러면 동의하지 않을 때는?: 반대의 표현)

	Not Formal (허물없는 표현) (for friends)	**Formal** (예의를 갖춘 표현) (for elders / important people)
weakly disagree → strongly disagree	• That's a terrible idea! • You have to be kidding! • I don't think so at all. • No way. • Are you joking? • I don't think so. • Not necessarily. • That's not always the case. • We are on different sides on this one.	• With all due respect, I disagree. • I'm of a different opinion. • While I respect your opinion, I think differently. • I'm afraid that I have to disagree. • I'm sorry but I don't think that's right. • While possible, I am unsure if I agree.

Opinion	Agreement (Your Answers)

I think that going to Thailand would be a lot of fun.

Partner Practice: With a partner or partners, respond to the opinions below:

1. Korea is the best country.
2. You should eat kimchi every day.
3. There are too many coffee shops.
4. Hongdae dance clubs are great!
5. English class is fun.
6. I like summer best.
7. Learning English is important.
8. We should eat more vegetables.
9. Smoking is bad.
10. You shouldn't marry until after you are 27 years old.

Grammar Focus 1: *The Simple Present*

How to use the simple present (chapter 7), when talking about travel.

We use the simple present to show an action that is repeated. Here are some important verbs we can use when discussing travel plans. Can you write these in Korean?

English	Korean	English	Korean
book (a flight, a hotel, etc.)	예약하다	wait	
go		swim	
travel		hike	
depart		sunbathe	
arrive		shop	
drive		visit	
take (a boat / a train, etc.)		relax	

Exercise 1 *Don't forget, the verb conjugates depending on the type of subject. Complete the table with the correct forms of the verbs from previous page .*

기억해야 할 것은 동사는 주어의 형태에 따라 변화한다는 것입니다.
앞 페이지의 동사들의 정확한 형태로 다음 도표를 채워 보세요.

Pronoun	verb		Pronoun	verb	
I You We They	book ______ ______ ______ ______ ______ ______ ______ ______	______ ______ ______ ______ ______ ______ ______ ______	He She It	books ______ ______ ______ ______ ______ ______ ______ ______	______ ______ ______ ______ ______ ______ ______ ______

Present Simple Negative:

When making the negative (NOT) or questions with HE / SHE / IT → S, you must remember the new rules.

- Rule 1: HE / SHE / IT ➡ S / ES / IES
- Rule 2: S loves "DO"

How do you add "not" to this sentence?

I am tired. → I am not tired. (this is easy because it is the "be" verb)

I play tennis → I play not tennis ✘ I not play tennis ✘

→ I do not play tennis ✔ I don't play tennis ✔

So, when making (NOT) sentences with no "be" verb, we use DO!

Exercise 2 *Make negative sentences with the following sentences using "DON'T":*

1. We ____________ *(not walk)* home from school.
2. They ____________ *(not drink)* diet sodas.
3. You ____________ *(not play)* ping pong.
4. I ____________ *(not play)* tennis every Saturday.
5. We ____________ *(not dance)* very well.
6. My neighbors ____________ *(not work)* at the hospital.
7. They ____________ *(not eat)* fish.

I YOU WE THEY	} DON'T

8. The students __________ *(not study)* for their tests.

9. I __________ *(not live)* in California.

10. The stores usually __________ *(not close)* at 10 p.m.

Exercise 3 *Make negative sentences with the following sentences using "DOESN'T":*

NOTE: ONLY 1 "S"   He doesn't plays. ✘   *He doesn't play.* ✔

1. She ______________ *(not watch)* T.V.
2. He ______________ *(not talk)* quietly in class.
3. It ______________ *(not eat)* breakfast in the morning.
4. George ______________ *(not like)* playing computer.
5. He ______________ *(not march)* .
6. My neighbor ______________ *(not work)* at the hospital.
7. He ______________ *(not eat)* fish.
8. The student ______________ *(not study)* for his/her tests.
9. It ______________ *(not live)* in California.
10. The store usually ______________ *(not close)* at 10 p.m.

HE SHE IT	DOESN'T

Exercise 4 *Make the sentences using the negative (NOT).*

1. (he/not go to school every day): He doesn't go to school every day.
2. (I/not like swimming): ______________________________
3. (you/not play badminton on Saturdays): ______________________________
4. (the class/not begin at 9 a.m.): ______________________________
5. (they/not go to the cinema): ______________________________
6. (she/not love chocolate): ______________________________
7. (they/not live in London): ______________________________
8. (he/not work in a restaurant): ______________________________
9. (Luke/not play the guitar): ______________________________
10. (we/not cook): ______________________________
11. (he/not clean my bedroom): ______________________________

Dialogue B:

Hye-jin: Hi Ji-hye! How are your vacation plans? 1. Going somewhere nice?

Ji-hye: Yes. As you probably know, we travel to Busan every summer.

Hye-jin: Every summer? Isn't that boring?

Ji-hye: No, I do lots of fun stuff with my sister. We usually go shopping and visit friends. My father and brother always swim and sunbathe at the beach.

Hye-jin: What about your mother?

Ji-hye: She 2. rarely does anything. She just relaxes. She sometimes takes a boat ride.

Hye-jin: You should check out the seafood barbecue restaurants. They are great.

Ji-hye: Oh. I never eat seafood. I always feel sick afterwards.

Hye-jin: Well, you must be excited about the trip. When will you leave?

Ji-hye: We leave tomorrow from Seoul Station on the KTX at 9:15.

Hye-jin: Wow! 3. You had better get packing!

Ji-hye: What about you? What are your plans?

Hye-jin: I don't have any plans yet. We usually make plans 4. at the last minute. It is always a surprise, but it usually works out well.

Ji-hye: Wow! Well I hope you have a great time. Oops… look at the time. I have to go. 5. Safe travels!

Substitution Drill: Use the following responses in the above conversation. Practice each with a partner two times. Try to pronounce each word correctly.

		A	B
1.	Going somewhere nice?	Where are you going?	Do you have a good place to travel to?
2.	rarely does anything.	doesn't do very much.	takes it easy.
3.	You had better get packing!	You should start getting ready!	You should be preparing!
4.	at the last minute.	when there is no more time to decide.	without much time remaining.
5.	Safe travels!	Have a good trip!	Have a good vacation.

Read the dialogue with a partner, then try to answer these questions.

1. Where (is) Ji-hye going on vacation?

   Ji-hye is going to ____________ .

> Please look at the difference between "be" verb and "do" verb!
> "be"동사와 "do"동사의 차이를 살펴보세요.

2. What do(es) Ji-hye usually do on vacation?

   She usually goes to ____________ and ____________ .
   (place) (activity)

3. What does Ji-hye's mother do?

   Her mother always ____________ and sometimes ____________ .
   (activity) (activity)

Conversation Corner: *Having to Choose*

Sometimes, you are asked to make a decision, or to add to a decision based on your opinion. When this happens, you can use the following expressions.

때로는 결정을 해야 하거나 당신의 견해를 바탕으로 결정을 해야 할 때가 있습니다. 이런 경우에는 다음의 표현을 사용할 수 있습니다.

If Given 2 Good Options and you like both 2개의 좋은 선택 모두를 당신이 좋아할 때	• I could go either way on that. • I like both ideas. • I'm easy. Both are good. • Whichever. Both sound good. • I'm up for either.
If given more than two options 2개 이상의 선택이 주어질 때	• I'm up for anything. • I'm fine with anything. • Whatever you think. • I'll go with whatever you decide. • I'm easy. Everything sounds good.
If asked to make a choice when you don't have enough information. 충분한 정보가 주어지지 않은 상태에서 결정을 해야 할 때	• Actually, I'm not sure. I'll let you decide. • I'll go along with what you all decide. • Hmm, I really don't have enough information to have an opinion. Sorry. • I don't know enough to even guess. I trust your decision.

Answer the following questions with the appropriate response?

Would you like to get coffee or ice cream? ________________________________ .

Which club do you think is best? ________________________________ .

We can go up to the university area. We can eat, dance, drink, and even find a singing room there.

How does that sound to everyone? ________________________________ .

What do you think about our classes? ________________________________ .

I could go for pizza, pasta, sandwiches, or burgers. What about you? ________________ .

PARTNER WORK: (상대방 역할)

Finish the sentences and then ask your partner.

I think we should go to ____________ (place) or ____________ (place) Friday night? How about you?

(Lunch Time) Let's go to ____________ (restaurant). Or we could get ____________ (food) at ____________ (restaurant).

Who would you rather date, ____________ (famous person) or ____________ (famous person)?

What kind of movie do you want to see? There is a ____________ (movie type) movie or a ____________ (movie type).

> For movie type examples, look at the beginning of unit 7

Grammar Focus 2: *Adverbs of Frequency*

Adverbs of frequency are very useful words, and change the meaning of sentences in a very powerful way.

I brush my teeth.

Now look what happens when we add an adverb of frequency…

I **never** brush my teeth.

That has a very different meaning, doesn't it?
The chart on the next page shows some common adverbs, and their approximate frequency value in the form of percentage.

never	hardly ever / rarely	seldom	sometimes	often / frequently	usually	always
0%	20%	35%	50%	65%	80%	100%

There are TWO places where we use "Adverbs of Frequency"

1) Between Subject and Verb (← not "be" verb):

subject	frequency adverb	verb
I	always	study.
He	always	**studies.**

2) After "be" verb:

subject	be verb	frequency adverb	
I	**am**	always	late.
He	**is**	always	late.
You	**are**	always	late.

Exercise 5 *Put the adverb of frequency in the parentheses (   ) in the correct place in the sentence with an arrow (→).*

Ex. She is **always** late. (always)

1. I	am	tired. (sometimes)	**2.** He	goes	hiking. (never)
3. They	play	soccer. (often)	**4.** You	are	funny. (usually)
5. She	is	sick. (seldom)	**6.** You	work	hard. (often)
7. Brenda	walks	to school. (always)	**8.** They	listen	to music. (never)
9. I	help	older people. (always)	**10.** It	is	friendly. (usually)

Adverbs of Frequency are used with the question "HOW OFTEN... ?

Ex. How often do you eat in a restaurant?
B. Rarely.
(B. I rarely eat in a restaurant.)

> One word answers are common in real dialogues. But you need to practice the full sentences and grammar. USE FULL SENTENCES when talking and ON TEST.

Exercise 6 *Look at the week schedule below and answer the questions about Akari Bano*

	Saturday	Sunday	Monday	Tuesday	Wednesday	Thursday	Friday
morning	sleep in late	sleep in late	cook breakfast	cook breakfast	cook breakfast	cook breakfast	cook breakfast
afternoon	play badminton	have coffee with friends	Go to English classes	Go to English classes	Go to English classes	Go to English classes	Go to English classes
evening	eat out with family, do homework	eat out with family, do homework	Cook dinner, do homework	Cook dinner, do homework	Cook dinner, do homework	Cook dinner, do homework	Cook dinner, do homework
night	watch the late movie	Go to bed early	Go to bed early	Go to bed early	Go to bed early	Go to bed early	take a hot bath and read a book

1. How often does she work?
   She ________ works.
2. How often does she play soccer?
   She ________ plays soccer.
3. How often does she go to bed early?
   She ________ goes to bed early.
4. How often does she watch the late movie?
   She ________ watches the late movie.
5. How often does she sleep in late?
   She ________ sleeps in late.
6. How often does she do homework?
   She ________ does homework.
7. How often does she dance in Hongdae?
   She ________ dances in Hongdae.
8. How often does she drink coffee with friends?
   She ________ drinks coffee with friends.
9. How often does she read a book?
   She ________ reads a book.
10. How often does she cook breakfast and dinner?
    She ________ cooks breakfast and dinner.

Exercise 7 *Practice these questions with your partner. Write your partner's responses with HE / SHE / IT = S*

		Your	Your partner
1	How often do you study in the library?	I ________ study in the library.	He / She ________ studies in the library.
2	How often do you watch the news?	I ________ watch the news.	He / She ________ watches the news.
3	How often are you tired in class?	I am ________ tired in class.	He / She is ________ tired in class.
4	How often do you drink coffee with friends?	I ________ ________.	He / She ________ ________.
5	How often do you watch movies at the cinema?	I ________ ________.	He / She ________ ________.
6	How often do you listen to music?	I ________ ________.	He / She ________ ________.
7	How often do you eat kimbab from GS 25?	I ________ ________.	He / She ________ ________.

MORE WAYS OF TALKING ABOUT FREQUENCY:

Look at this sentence: I *always* brush my teeth.
What does this mean? Am I constantly brushing my teeth and never stopping? Does this mean everyday, or more… or less? It is very unclear. So we use other words to describe this routine action. Study the words below.
위 문장의 의미는 무엇일까요? 내가 쉬지 않고 이를 끊임없이 닦는다는 의미인가요? 매일 아니면 더 또는 덜? 매우 불분명합니다. 그래서 이런 일상적인 행동을 표현할 때에는 다른 단어를 사용합니다. 아래 단어들을 보세요.

		Other words:
1 X = once a…	day	daily / everyday
2 X = twice a…	week	weekly / every week
3 X = three times a…	month	Saturdays / every Saturday
4 X = four times a…	year	mornings / every morning
5 X = five times a…	hour	

Ex. I brush my teeth three times a day.
I brush my teeth everyday.
➡ These sentences are clearer and easier to understand. "I always brush my teeth" is not wrong, but less accurate. In this case, "three times a day" is better suited.

Exercise 8 *Look at the week schedule below and answer the questions about Akari USING "once a week"/"twice a week"/"five times a week"/"never"/or "everyday".*

	Saturday	Sunday	Monday	Tuesday	Wednesday	Thursday	Friday
morning	sleep in late	sleep in late	cook breakfast	cook breakfast	cook breakfast	cook breakfast	cook breakfast
afternoon	play badminton	have coffee with friends	Go to English classes	Go to English classes	Go to English classes	Go to English classes	Go to English classes
evening	eat out with family, do homework	eat out with family, do homework	Cook dinner, do homework	Cook dinner, do homework	Cook dinner, do homework	Cook dinner, do homework	Cook dinner, do homework
night	watch the late movie	Go to bed early	Go to bed early	Go to bed early	Go to bed early	Go to bed early	take a hot bath and read a book

Ex. How often does she watch T.V. with her family?

She watches T.V. with her family once a week.

1. How often does she work? She works ______________________.
2. How often does she play soccer? She ______________ plays soccer.
3. How often does she go to bed early? She goes to bed early ______________.
4. How often does she cook breakfast? She cooks breakfast ______________.
5. How often does she sleep in late? She sleeps in late ______________.
6. How often does she do homework? She does homework ______________.
7. How often does she dance in Hongdae? She ______________ dances in Hongdae.
8. How often does she drink coffee with friends?

   She drinks coffee with friends ______________________.

TOEIC VOCABULARY

Read the following common TOEIC words. Memorize so that you can do well on the TOEIC. Write the Korean and English below in the blanks two times to help you learn.

lawyer: 변호사.
Her dream was to become a lawyer.
(그녀의 꿈은 변호사가 되는 것이었다.)

_______ /_______ _______ /_______

prove: 증명하다.
To my surprise, the rumor proved to be true.
(놀랍게도 소문은 사실로 판명되었다.)

_______ /_______ _______ /_______

leave: 떠나다.
I want you to leave right now.
(지금 당장 나가주십시오.)

_______ /_______ _______ /_______

particular: 특별한.
I have nothing to do in particular tomorrow.
(내일은 특별히 할 것이 없다.)

_______ /_______ _______ /_______

lose: 잃다.
You have no time to lose.
(너는 우물쭈물할 틈이 없어.)

_______ /_______ _______ /_______

respect: 존경하다.
We must respect other senior citizens as well as our parents.
(부모님은 물론이고 다른 어르신들도 존경해야 한다.)

_______ /_______ _______ /_______

stay: 머무르다.
Mother made me stay home at any rate.
(어머니는 아무튼지 나를 집에 있게 했다.)

_______ /_______ _______ /_______

will: 의지.
She was made to go out with him against her will.
(그녀는 자신의 의지와 달리 그와 사귀어야 했다.)

_______ /_______ _______ /_______

rich: 부유한.
He seems to have been rich when young.
(그는 젊었을 때 부유했었던 것 같다.)

_______ /_______ _______ /_______

worse: 더 나쁜.
To make matters worse, I've lost my watch.
(설상가상으로 시계까지 잃어버렸다.)

_______ /_______ _______ /_______

stone: 돌.
A rolling stone gathers no moss.
(구르는 돌에는 이끼가 끼지 않는다.)

_______ /_______ _______ /_______

consider: 고려하다.
All things considered, he was released.
(모든 것을 고려하여 그는 석방되었다.)

_______ /_______ _______ /_______

strictly: 엄격하게.
Strictly speaking, you didn't pass the exam.
(엄격히 말해서 너는 시험에 통과하지 못했다.)

_______ /_______ _______ /_______

learn: 배우다.
Learning is one thing; teaching is another.
(배우는 것과 가르치는 것은 전혀 별개의 것이다.)

_______ /_______ _______ /_______

mind: 꺼려하다.
Would you mind my staying here?
(여기 좀 있어도 될까요?)

_______ /_______ _______ /_______

occasion: 경우.
Face the music at any occasion.
(어떤 경우라도 시련을 피하지 말아라.)

_______ /_______ _______ /_______

regards: 안부.
Give my best regards to your parents.
(부모님께 제 안부를 전해 주세요.)

__________ /__________ __________ /__________

know: 알다.
I don't know why not.
(당연하지요.)

__________ /__________ __________ /__________

keep: 계속하다.
Keep in touch with me just in case.
(혹시 모르니 계속 저와 연락하세요.)

__________ /__________ __________ /__________

again: 다시.
I look forward to seeing you again.
(다시 만나기를 고대합니다.)

__________ /__________ __________ /__________

far: 먼.
How far is it from here?
(여기서 얼마나 먼가요?)

__________ /__________ __________ /__________

traffic: 교통.
The traffic is bumper to bumper.
(도로가 꽉 막혔네요.)

__________ /__________ __________ /__________

free: 한가로운.
Will you be free this weekend?
(이번 주말 시간 있으세요?)

__________ /__________ __________ /__________

home: 가정.
Make yourself at home.
(편히 지내세요.)

__________ /__________ __________ /__________

enjoy: 즐기다.
I enjoyed myself today.
(오늘 즐거웠습니다.)

__________ /__________ __________ /__________

grateful: 감사하는.
I'm really grateful to you.
(정말 감사합니다.)

__________ /__________ __________ /__________

take: (시간이) 걸리다.
This won't take a long time.
(오래 걸리지는 않을 것입니다.)

__________ /__________ __________ /__________

afraid: 유감스러운.
I'm afraid I'm running late.
(늦을 것 같습니다.)

__________ /__________ __________ /__________

disturb: 방해하다.
Am I disturbing you?
(제가 방해가 되나요?)

__________ /__________ __________ /__________

favor: 호의, 부탁.
Could you do me a favor?
(도와주실 수 있으십니까?)

__________ /__________ __________ /__________

UNIT

9 At the Store

Review Questions:

- Where have you travelled? ______________________________.
- What is your hobby? ______________________________.
- Where would you like to travel, if you had the time and money? ______________.
- What is your favorite day? ______________________________.
- What is your favorite month? ______________________________.

Warm-up Questions:

Practice the questions and answers with your partner.

25) What is the most beautiful place you know?

The most beautiful place I know is

______________________________.
(place name)

DISCUSSION: Before answering the next question, let's discuss as a class and write answers down in the box below why ENGLISH is important.

다음 질문에 답하기 전에 어째서 영어가 중요한 것인지를 학급 전체가 토론을 해 보고 아래 상자 안에 답을 써 봅시다.

-
-
-
-

26) Why do you study English?

I study English because

______________________________.

27) What was your favorite subject in high school?

My favorite subject was

______________________________.

Subject: Write the Korean:
Math:
Social Studies:
English:
P.E.:
Science:
Art:
Music:
Korean:
History:
Geography:

Dialogue A:

Talk about the picture.

- Where are they?
- What are they doing?
- What can you see?

1– A: Do you like shopping for electronics?
B: Yes, I do./No, I don't.
A: Why?
B: Because…

Shop assistant: Good afternoon. Do you need any help to find anything?

Ricardo: That would be great. 1. I'm interested in buying a new smartphone, but there are so many to choose from.

Shop assistant: Do you have a brand 2. that you prefer?

Ricardo: I heard that the Samsung products are all very good, 3. but I don't mind. I just want a good price. Do you have anything that is cheap?

Shop assistant: Ok, I see. What do you think about this smartphone? It has many great features and it has a big screen.

Ricardo: How much is it?

Shop assistant: It is 499,000 won. It's a great deal!
(four hundred ninety-nine thousand won)

Ricardo: Wow! That is so expensive! 4. I don't have that much money. Do you have any cheaper cell phones? Maybe a cell phone that is on sale?

Shop assistant: Yes, we do. Look at this cell phone. It is on sale this week only. It has a 30% discount so it costs only 249,000 won. What do you think?
(two hundred forty-nine thousand won)

Ricardo: 5. That's a great deal. I'll take it.

Substitution Drill: Use the following responses in the above conversation. Practice each with a partner two times. Try to pronounce each word correctly.

		A	B
1.	I'm interested in buying	I'm considering buying	I'm thinking about getting
2.	that you prefer?	that you like more than others?	that you want especially?
3.	but I don't mind.	but I don't have a strong opinion.	it doesn't really matter.
4.	I don't have that much money.	That is not in my price range.	That's a bit too much for me right now.
5.	That's a great deal.	That is an excellent price.	I like that price.

VOCABULARY:

1– With a partner, match each word from the dialogue with a meaning below. The first one is done for you.

1. __E__ price
2. _____ bargain
3. _____ 20% off
4. _____ half price
5. _____ on sale
6. _____ expensive
7. _____ cheap

A. a great/affordable price.
B. costing a lot of money.
C. a reduction to the usual price.
D. 50% off the original price.
E. the amount of money you pay for something.
F. a 20% discount off the original price.
G. costing a little money.

2– Ask your partner the questions. Read the answers and then make your own.

1. When did you last get a bargain?

   Ex. I got a bargain when I bought a new T.V. I got 30% off!

   ____.

2. What is something expensive that you own?

   Ex. My watch is very expensive. It cost 200,000 won.

   ____.

Conversation Corner: *Practice the questions and answers with your partner.*

QUESTION	RESPONSE
A. How much is it?	A. It's 15,000 won.
B. Is this expensive?	B. Yes, it is.
C. Is that cheap?	C. No, it isn't.
D. Do you have a sale on?	D. Yes, we do / No, we don't.
E. Is there a discount on this?	E. Yes, there is.
F. What is the discount?	F. It's 20%.

SAYING NUMBERS:

English is actually easier than Korean because we have only three place values (one-ten-hundred) whereas Korean has five place values (일–십–백–천–만). Practice writing and saying the numbers. Your teacher will give you spelling whenever necessary.

Let's start easy: 1 (one) 10 (ten) 100 (hundred)

132: one hundred "and" thirty-two / one hundred thirty-two / a hundred and thirty-two	**455:** four hundred and fifty-five four hundred fifty-five.	**980:** ______
567: ______	**703:** ______	**340:** ______
1,176: one thousand one hundred and seventy-six one thousand one hundred seventy-six	**2,360:** ______	**9,706:** ______
110,450: one hundred and ten thousand, four hundred and fifty. a hundred and ten thousand, four hundred and fifty.	**270,670:** ______	**600,600:** ______
1,400,190: one million, four hundred thousand, one hundred and ninety one million, four hundred thousand, one hundred ninety.	**1,500,000:** ______	**2,780,900:** ______

When talking about dollars($) and cents(¢), we use the "and" differently.	\$112.36 One hundred twelve dollars AND thirty-six cents.	\$1,900.99 One thousand nine hundred dollars AND ninety-nine cents.

MATCHING:

Number		Number written
1,505,005	______	A. seven million, eight hundred and ninety-two thousand, four hundred and fifty.
1,515,050	______	B. four hundred and fifty-seven thousand, nine hundred and nine.
7,892,450	______	C. Seven thousand eight hundred ninety-two dollars and forty-five cents.
7,982,450	______	D. four million, five hundred and seventy thousand, nine hundred.
$4,570.90	______	E. one million, five hundred and five thousand five hundred.
1,505,500	______	F. seven million, nine hundred and eighty-two thousand, four hundred and fifty.
457,990	______	G. one million, five hundred and fifteen thousand, fifty.
457,909	______	H. one million, five hundred and five thousand and five.
4,570,900	______	I. Four thousand five hundred and seventy dollars and ninety cents.
$7,892.45	______	J. four hundred and fifty-seven thousand, nine hundred and ninety.

Grammar Focus 1: *Present simple –Making Questions*

We use the simple present for 2 reasons.

1. To talk about things that are generally true.	**2.** To talk about habits and routines.
I speak Korean. *He speaks Korean.*	*I get up at 7 a.m. every day.* *She gets up at 7 a.m. every day.*

*Remember... if there is NO WWWWWH (who, what, where, why, when, how), then the answer is usually YES or NO!

Pronoun	Affirmative	Negative(not)	Inquisitive?(Question)	
I You We They	play go eat study do drink	don't play don't go don't eat don't study don't do don't drink	Do I play... ? Do you go... ? Do we eat... ? Do they study... ? Do I do... ? Do you drink... ?	Yes, I do. / No, I don't. Yes, you do. / No, you don't. Yes, we do. / No, we don't. Yes they do. / No, they don't. Yes, I do. / No, I don't. Yes, you do. / No, you don't.
He She It (+S)	plays goes eats studies does drinks	doesn't play doesn't go doesn't eat doesn't study doesn't do doesn't drink	Does he play... ? Does she go... ? Does it eat... ? Does he study... ? Does she do... ? Does it drink... ?	Yes, he does. / No, he doesn't. Yes, she does. / No, she doesn't. Yes, it does. / No, it doesn't. Yes, he does. / No, he doesn't. Yes, she does. / No, she doesn't. Yes, it does. / No, it doesn't.

Exercise 1 *Look at the pictures then answer the questions.*

1. 	Does he play the piano after university? Yes, he does.
2. 	Does Katie study English on Fridays? No, ____________ . She ____________ to art class on Fridays.
3. 	Does Ricardo play soccer at 10 a.m. on Saturdays? Yes, ______________________ .
4. 	Do they eat lunch at 1 p.m.? No, ____________ . They ____________ lunch at 12 p.m.
5. 	Do we drive to work? Yes, ______________________ .
6. 	Does it sleep on the sofa? No, ____________ . It ____________ on the floor.

Exercise 2 *Look at the pictures then answer the questions.*

	George	Mark	Brenda	Billy	Sarah	Jennifer
swim	▯	▯	X	X	▯	▯
dance on Friday night	▯	X	▯	▯	▯	X
speak Korean	X	X	▯	▯	X	▯
work part-time	X	▯	▯	▯	X	X
save money	▯	X	X	X	▯	▯
speak English well	X	▯	X	X	X	▯

▯ → yes
X → no

1. Do Brenda and Sarah speak English well? No, they don't.
2. ________ George work part-time? ________ , ________ ________ .
3. ________ Billy dance on Friday night? ________ , ________ ________ .
4. ________ Sarah and Jennifer save money? ________ , ________ ________ .
5. ________ George and Mark swim? ________ , ________ ________ .
6. ________ Brenda speak English well? ________ , ________ ________ .
7. ________ Billy and Brenda swim? ________ , ________ ________ .
8. ________ Sarah dance on Friday night? ________ , ________ ________ .
9. ________ Jennifer work part-time? ________ , ________ ________ .
10. ________ Mark and Sarah speak Korean? ________ , ________ ________ .

Exercise 3 *Write complete questions and answers for the following:*

1. (you/like cake?) (no)
   Do you like cake? No, I don't.
2. (she/live in Ilsan?) (yes)
   ________________________________ .
3. (they/hate studying?) (no)
   ________________________________ .
4. (you/eat kimchi every morning?) (yes)
   ________________________________ .
5. (he/play soccer on Sundays?) (yes)
   ________________________________ .
6. (he/study nursing?) (no)
   ________________________________ .

7. (I/take vitamins?) (yes)

______________________________ .

8. (you/go shopping at Shinsegae?) (no)

______________________________ .

9. (they smoke?) (no)

______________________________ .

10. (she/work in a bakery?) (yes)

______________________________ .

GROUP WORK: Go around the room and ask about what other students do.

ASK "Do you…" Write "Yes, he / she does." Or "No, he / she doesn't."

Name (English)	swim	drive a car	run fast	sing well	cook
__________					
__________					
__________					
__________					
__________					
__________					
__________					
__________					
__________					
__________					

Dialogue B: *Talking about getting deals.*

Jenny: 1. What do you think about these shoes?

Akari: Oh. I like them. They are so cute. How much are they?

Jenny: The tag says 189,000 won. So… about $180 or so. I think it is a bit too expensive but maybe I can afford it.

Akari: Let's keep looking. I'm sure we'll find something cheaper and 2. just as nice.

Jenny: Sure. Let's try over there.

Akari: Here is a another cute pair. What do you think?

Jenny: Hmm. I like them but I wonder if they come in a different color. (To clerk) Excuse me, do you know if these come in black or dark blue?

Clerk: Yes, they come in blue. 3. Would you like me to get them for you?

Jenny: That would be great.

Clerk: (comes back). The biggest size is 250 mm. What size do you need?

Jenny: I need 255 mm, but let me try them on. (tries shoes on). 4. No, they don't fit. I guess me and my big feet will shop online.

Akari: That's too bad. Let me try them on!

Jenny: Wow. They look good on you! You should buy them.

Akari: I can't afford new shoes right now. I'm just 5. window shopping.

Substitution Drill: Use the following responses in the above conversation. Practice each with a partner two times. Try to pronounce each word correctly.

		A	B
1.	What do you think about	What's your opinion of	Do you like
2.	just as nice.	as good as those ones.	that look just as good on you.
3.	Would you like me to get them for you?	Shall I bring them out?	Do you want me to get them?
4.	No, they don't fit.	They are too small.	a bit too tight for me.
5.	window shopping.	looking around.	looking but not buying.

Conversation Corner: *Getting what you want!*

Asking about items: (물건에 대해 질문하기)

- Can you help me? I am looking for…
  I want to buy…
- Do you have this / these in…

Size(치수)	Color(색상)	Style(스타일)
• a smaller size?	• the color blue?	• striped pattern?
• in size 6?	• any other colors?	• with a different picture?
• in a larger size?	• (color) ?	• with long sleeves?
		• a bit longer in front?

Asking about prices? (가격에 대해 질문하기)

- Do you have anything like this, but cheaper?
- Do you have anything in the price range of (money)?
  Ex. Do you have anything in the price range of 40,000 won?
- Is there anything on sale right now?
- Is there a sale coming soon?
- Is this the best price you can give me?

Trying it on: (입어보기)

- Is it possible to try it on first?
- May I try this on?
- Where is the dressing room?

Buying the item: (물건 구매하기)

- I'll take it.
- OK, I'll buy it. How much is the total?
- Ring it up for me please.

Grammar Focus 2: *WWWWWH questions in the Present Simple*

Affirmative	WH question
• What **do** you usually do on the weekend?	• I usually **meet** my friends.
• Where **does** she go to university?	• She **goes** to university in Seoul.
• When **does** he leave for work?	• He **leaves** for work at 8 a.m.
• Why **do** they always get up at 6.30 a.m.?	• Because they **go** to work at 7.30 a.m.
• What **do** we do in English class?	• We **study** English.

REMEMBER: HE / SHE / IT ➡ S

Exercise 4 *Complete the sentences with the correct form of the verb.*

1. What time do you usually get up? I usually ________ up at 6 a.m.
2. What time does Rachel usually eat lunch? She usually ________ lunch at 12.30 p.m.
3. When do they watch movies? They ________ movies on Fridays.
4. What time does Matt leave for work every day? He ________ for work at 8 a.m. every day.
5. What time do we study English? We ________ English at 10 a.m.
6. Where does Jill work? She ________ at Pizza Hut.
7. How do you get to university? I ________ to university by shuttle bus.
8. Where does he live? He ________ in Uijeongbu.
9. Who do you live with? I ________ with my father, mother and younger sister.
10. How do they feel? They ________ angry at the noisy students.

Exercise 5 *Now make questions*

1. (where/you/go to school?) Where do you go to school?
2. (what/you/do?) ________________
3. (where/ John/come from?) ________________
4. (how long/it/take from Seoul to Busan?) ________________

5. (when/she/go to the cinema?) ______________________

6. (what/he/do in the morning?) ______________________

7. (when/you/get up?) ______________________

8. (where/you/study English?) ______________________

9. (what game/he/play?) ______________________

10. (what sport/you/play?) ______________________

Exercise 6 *Backward Build-up: Make the questions! Use the underlined answers.*

1. Where does he live?
   He lives in Suwon.
2. ______________________?
   He eats pizza.
3. ______________________?
   I love my girlfriend.
4. ______________________?
   They work at GS 25.
5. ______________________?
   We play soccer on Sunday.
6. ______________________?
   You get to university by car.
7. ______________________?
   He studies Korean and English.
8. ______________________?
   It hides under the stairs.
9. ______________________?
   I sleep in class because I am tired.
10. ______________________?
    He goes to bed at 11:00 p.m.

TOEIC VOCABULARY

Read the following common TOEIC words. Memorize so that you can do well on the TOEIC. Write the Korean and English below in the blanks two times to help you learn.

allow: 허락하다.
Swimming is not allowed here.
(이 곳에서는 수영을 할 수 없습니다.)

__________ /__________ __________ /__________

arrange: 정리하다, 계획을 세우다.
The chairs are arranged around the table.
(탁자 근처에 의자가 정리되어 있다.)

__________ /__________ __________ /__________

repair: 수리하다.
The road is being repaired.
(도로 수리 중이다.)

__________ /__________ __________ /__________

cost: 비용이 들다.
How much does it cost?
(얼마인가요?)

__________ /__________ __________ /__________

take: 시간이 걸리다.
How long will it take?
(시간이 얼마나 걸릴까요?)

__________ /__________ __________ /__________

get to: 도착하다.
How did she get to New York?
(그녀는 뉴욕에 어떻게 갔습니까?)

__________ /__________ __________ /__________

fix: 고치다.
Who should I ask to fix the engine?
(누구에게 엔진을 수리해 달라고 해야 합니까?)

__________ /__________ __________ /__________

put: 두다, 놓다.
Where can we put these boxes?
(이 상자들을 어디에 놓을까요?)

__________ /__________ __________ /__________

hold: 개최하다, 보유하다, 주장하다.
Where is this conversation being held?
(위 대화가 진행되는 장소가 어디인가요?)

__________ /__________ __________ /__________

develop: 개발하다, 발전하다.
What did he help to develop?
(그는 무엇을 개발하는데 도움을 주었습니까?)

__________ /__________ __________ /__________

offer: 제공하다.
What kind of seat is she offering?
(그녀는 어떤 종류의 좌석을 제공하고 있나요?)

__________ /__________ __________ /__________

ask: 요구하다, 묻다.
Customers are asked to give their names at the reception desk.
(고객들은 접수대에서 자신의 이름을 제시해야 합니다.)

__________ /__________ __________ /__________

deliver: 배달하다, 해방시키다, 분만하다.
Any furniture which is bought today will be delivered by next week.
(오늘 구매하는 모든 가구는 다음 주에 배달될 것입니다.)

__________ /__________ __________ /__________

require: 요구하다.
All students are required by school regulations to carry student card.
(모든 학생들은 학교 규정에 의거하여 학생증을 휴대해야 합니다.)

__________ /__________ __________ /__________

carry: 휴대하다, 옮기다.
What might happen if they don't carry their ID cards?
(신분증이 없으면 그들은 어떻게 되나요?)

__________ /__________ __________ /__________

infer: 유추하다, 추론하다.
What can we infer from this conversation?
(위 대화로부터 무엇을 유추할 수 있습니까?)
What can we infer about this place?
(위 장소에 대해 무엇을 유추할 수 있습니까?)
What can be inferred from this conversation?
(위 대화로부터 무엇을 유추할 수 있습니까?)

__________ /__________ __________ /__________

cancel: 취소하다.
Why does the flight have to be cancelled?
(비행이 취소된 이유는 무엇입니까?)

__________ /__________ __________ /__________

discuss: 토론하다.
What are they discussing?
(그들은 무엇을 토론하고 있습니까?)

__________ /__________ __________ /__________

run: 진행되다.
How long is the sale running?
(얼마나 오랫동안 판매가 진행됩니까?)

__________ /__________ __________ /__________

crash: 추락하다.
Where did the plane crash?
(비행기는 어디에서 추락했나요?)

__________ /__________ __________ /__________

connection: 관계.
What was Jane's connection with the company?
(Jane과 회사의 관계는 무엇입니까?)

__________ /__________ __________ /__________

state: 진술하다.
They showed us a new product, stating that it was the world best.
(그들은 우리에게 신제품을 보여주면서 세계 최고의 제품이라고 말했다.)

__________ /__________ __________ /__________

remind: 상기시키다.
This painting always reminds me of my mother.
(이 그림을 볼 때마다 어머니 생각이 난다.)

__________ /__________ __________ /__________

ban: 금지하다.
Smoking is banned in this foyer.
(휴게실에서는 금연입니다.)

__________ /__________ __________ /__________

quote: 인용하다.
The analyst is quoted as saying like that.
(분석가는 그렇게 말했다고 인용되었다.)

__________ /__________ __________ /__________

bring: 가져오다.
Don't forget to bring your own bottles.
(각자 마실 술을 가져오는 것을 잊지 마세요.)

__________ /__________ __________ /__________

fund: 자금, 자금을 충당하다.
How will you fund the new construction?
(당신은 신규 건설 자금을 어떻게 충당할 예정입니까?)

__________ /__________ __________ /__________

let: 허락하다.
Don't let it go unnoticed.
(무심하게 방치하지 마세요.)

__________ /__________ __________ /__________

prefer: 선호하다.
Many people prefer to go shopping at KBT Mall.
(많은 사람들이 KBT 시장에서 장보기를 선호합니다.)

__________ /__________ __________ /__________

submit: 제출하다.
Don't forget to submit your assignment within the deadline?
(마감일 이내에 과제 제출하는 것을 잊지 마세요.)

__________ /__________ __________ /__________

TOEIC GRAMMAR EXERCISES:

Choose the correct answer. Some of the grammar has advanced rules.
We are hoping that by exposure, we can expand on your knowledge base.

1) How often do you go to Shinsaegae to shop?
A) Yes, I like to shop at Shinsaegae.
B) The clothes there are so nice.
C) About twice a month, if I can afford it.
D) I shop too much.
There is no more room in my closet.

2) My neighbor ______ the violin every chance he gets. If you listen carefully, he ______ the violin right now. He plays beautifully.
A) plays / plays B) is playing / plays
C) plays / is playing D) is playing / is playing

3) I usually ______ late for class.
A) come B) am coming
C) comes D) coming

4) She ______ often late for class.
A) comes B) is coming
C) is D) come

5) Please hold. He ______ to a client.
A) is talking B) talks
C) talk D) don't talk

6) Turn off the T.V. right now.
You ______ it anyway.
A) isn't watching B) aren't seeing
C) aren't watching D) can't seeing

7) He ______ seafood.
He always says no when I offer him some.
A) isn't liking B) don't like
C) don't likes D) doesn't like

8) ______ you ______ the movie? You look bored.
A) Do / enjoy B) Does / enjoy
C) Are / enjoy D) Are / enjoying

9) ______ he often ______ football? He looks very athletic.
A) Do / play B) Does / play
C) Is / playing D) Doesn't / plays

10) A: ______ do you go to bed early?
B: Hmm... I guess I rarely go to bed early.
I like late night T.V.
A) What B) What time
C) How much D) How often

11) ______ are you going? The show is about to start.
A) What B) How much
C) Where D) Who

12) A: Where ______ it ______?
B: It sleeps on that pillow over there.
A) is / sleeping B) do / sleep
C) does / sleeping D) does / sleep

13) Do you walk to school?
A) No, you do. B) No, I do.
C) Yes, I do. D) Yes, you don't.

14) Do Peter and Mary take dance lessons?
A) Yes, he does. B) Yes, she does.
C) No, they doesn't. D) No, they don't.

15) Are you practicing your English speaking?
A) Yes, I am. B) No, I amn't.
C) No, I don't. D) No, you don't.

UNIT

10 What Do You Think?

Review Questions:

- What is your favorite subject? My favorite subject is ____________________ .
- Where would you like to travel, if you had time and money?
  I would travel to ____________________ .
- What kinds of movies do you like to watch? I like to watch ____________________ .
- When is your birthday? ____________________ .
- What do you want to be in the future? ____________________ .

Warm-up Questions:

28) Do you think English is important? Why?

Yes, I do. I think it's important for

____________________ .

> Ex. For graduating university
> For getting a job
> For studying abroad
> For travelling

29) Why is learning English difficult?

Learning English is difficult because

____________________ .

> Ex. I am shy.
> It's not my first language.
> I don't live in an English-speaking country.

30) How will you study English over vacation?

I will ____________________ .

I won't ____________________ .

> Ex. I will learn more words.
> I will practice reading.
> I will watch English dramas.
> I will make an English-speaking friend.

Dialogue A: *What do you think?*

Interviewer: Your resume 1. is impressive, Ms. Kim. I have just a few more questions.

Min Ji: Of course.

Interviewer: I see that 2. your first language is not English. Do you think English is important, Ms. Kim?

Min Ji: Yes, I do.

Interviewer: Why?

Min Ji: I think English is important not only for school and work, but also for fun and travel. Learning English has allowed me to travel to so many places and meet so many new people.

Interviewer: Do you think learning English is difficult?

Min Ji: Yes, I do. 3. I admit that I still struggle, but it is worth it.

Interviewer: Why?

Min Ji: Well, first, it's not my first language. Second, it's difficult to practice English because no one in my family knows English. In Korea, there are not really any places where I can speak English.

Interviewer: Still, your English is very good. How do 4. you keep up with it?

Min Ji: I listen to English radio and watch English dramas. I email with English friends from all over the world. As well, there are a bunch of wonderful sites on the internet to help.

Interviewer: Thank you. You seem to be a good student. I hope you will also be a good worker. I'm happy to tell you that you will 5. be hired.

Min Ji: Really? Thank you very much!

Substitution Drill: Use the following responses in the above conversation. Practice each with a partner two times. Try to pronounce each word correctly.

		A	B
1.	is impressive	looks very good	is very interesting
2.	your first language is not English.	you are not a native speaker of English.	your first language is Korean, not English.
3.	I admit that I still struggle	I still have difficulties	I still find it difficult sometimes
4.	you keep up with it?	you continue to learn English?	you remember what you have learned?
5.	be hired.	get the job.	get the position you are applying for.

Exercise 1 *Listen to the dialogue carefully. Answer the true and false questions below. If it is false, write down the correct statement.*

대화를 잘 들어보세요. 참인지 거짓인지 표시하세요. 거짓이라면 정확한 내용을 써 보세요.

1. English is Ms. Kim's first language. T (F)

   English is not Ms. Kim's first language

2. Ms. Kim thinks English is important. T F

3. Ms. Kim doesn't think English is important for fun and travel. T F

4. The interviewer thinks Ms. Kim's English is very bad. T F

5. Ms. Kim won't get the job. T F

Conversation Corner: *Apologizing*

- Apologizing is a very "cultural topic". Just saying "I'm sorry" is often not enough.

  사과하는 것은 매우 "문화적인 주제"입니다. 단지 "미안해"라고만 말하는 것은 충분치 않습니다.
- An apology has 2 parts: 1) Knowing why you are sorry 2) Explaining why you are sorry.

  사과에는 두 부분이 있습니다. 1) 왜 유감인지를 인지하는 부분과 2) 왜 유감인지를 설명하는 부분입니다.

WORK IN A GROUP:
CAN YOU THINK OF EXAMPLES OF SMALL MISTAKES AND BIG MISTAKES?

조별로 해 보세요. 사소한 실수와 커다란 실수의 예를 생각해 볼 수 있을까요?

SMALL MISTAKES	BIG MISTAKES

little mistake → big mistake	First part… Apology	Second part… why
	• I'm deeply sorry for…	what I did. I hope you will forgive me.
	• I am truly sorry for…	what I said. I hope you understand.
	• I deeply apologize for…	what I didn't do. I will try harder in the future.
	• I'm sorry for…	(what I did). Please forget about it.
	• Sorry. I didn't mean to do that. • Sorry about that. • Sorry. My bad! • Oops. My mistake.	(not needed)

Work with a partner and your teacher:

What do you say when you step on another person's foot?

____ .

What do you say to the professor when you are late for class?

____ .

What do you say when you close the elevator door on someone?

____ .

What do you say when you spill hot coffee on your boss?

____ .

What do you say when you break a plate at your friend's house?

____ .

Grammar Focus 1: *Future with "Will"*

Pronoun	Affirmative	Negative(Not)	Question	
I	will go.	won't go. (will not go.)	Will I go?	Yes, I will. No, I won't. (No, I will not.)
You We They	will eat. will play. will sleep.	won't eat. (will not eat.) won't play. (will not play.) won't sleep. (will not sleep.)	Will you eat? Will we play? Will they sleep?	Yes, you will. No, you won't. (No, you will not) Yes, we will. No, we won't. (No, we will not.) Yes, they will. No, they won't. (No, they will not.)
He She It	will study. will read. will work.	won't study. (will not study.) won't read. (will not read.) won't work. (will not work.)	Will he study? Will she study? Will it go to work?	Yes, he will. No, he won't. (No, he will not.) Yes, she will. No, she won't. (No, she will not.) Yes, it will. No, it won't. (No, it will not.)

* will not = won't

** I / you / we / they / he / she / it are all the same ➡ WILL / WON'T

Exercise 2 *Complete each sentence using the verbs provided in parentheses and "WILL" or "WON'T".*

1. He ______________ a party tomorrow. (have)
2. We ______________ out next week. (not/go)
3. Johnny ______________ in a new movie. (be)
4. I ______________ Starcraft tonight. (not/play)
5. She ______________ him. (not/date)
6. Sue ______________ this weekend. (not/go jogging)
7. I ______________ late for class. (not/be)
8. It ______________ meat for lunch. (eat)
9. You ______________ hard for final tests. (study)
10. He ______________ the game. (win)
11. They ______________ home on Saturday. (not/stay)
12. I ______________ English well. (speak)

Exercise 3 *Correct the Sentences. Each of the sentences below has a mistake. Find the mistake and correct it.*

1. He will play not games tonight.

______________________ .

2. They will staying at home tonight.

______________________ .

3. She will is late for class.

______________________ .

4. I won't not eat kimchi tomorrow.

______________________ .

5. They go will to the beach next weekend.

______________________ .

6. He will eats pizza next week.

______________________ .

7. I willn't walk to university.

______________________ .

8. They not will take a bus.

______________________ .

9. You will to need some money.

______________________ .

10. It will plays with another dog.

______________________ .

Important Future Tense Time Phrases

tomorrow	tomorrow { morning / afternoon / evening / night	next { week / weekend / month (January, February, …) / year / holiday (Christmas, Chuseok, etc.)

CONTRACTION PRACTICE:

"Will" is often contracted to "'ll ". ("will"은 종종 " 'll"로 축약합니다.)

Ex. I will go home ➡ I'll go home.
He will play soccer ➡ He'll play soccer.

NOTE: There is nothing wrong with "I will" "He will".
"I will" "He will"로 표현해도 문제없습니다.
Using contractions can sometimes lead to errors so use them wisely.
축약된 표현을 사용하는 것은 가끔 오류를 일으킬 수 있으니 잘 사용하셔야 합니다.

I will → I'll	He will → He'll	They will → They'll
You will → You'll	She will → She'll	We will → We'll
	It will → It'll	

Exercise 4 *Make sentences with "will" or "won't" with the clues provided.*

1. (we/watch TV tomorrow)

____

2. (I/go fishing next vacation)

____

3. (she/not visit her grandmother next Christmas)

____

4. (they/not use the Internet this evening)

____

5. (you/go swimming next week)

____

6. (John/wait for the next bus)

____

7. (Lucy and Jill/not go out tonight)

____

8. (I/stay at home this Friday)

____

9. (he/drive his car to Daejeon next weekend)

____

10. (they/not have a party next Tuesday)

____

Exercise 5 *What about you? Fill in the chart with two things you POSSIBLY will do*

Tomorrow morning, I'll ______________________________ .

Next weekend, I'll ______________________________ .

Next vacation, I'll ______________________________ .

Next Chuseok, I'll ______________________________ .

Tomorrow night, I'll ______________________________ .

Share your answers with a partner. Take turns asking and answering.

NOTE 1: "WILL" implies possibility. It is often used when there are NO CERTAIN PLANS. Therefore, it is often used with "probably", "likely", and "maybe" to make PREDICTIONS.
"will"은 가능성을 암시합니다. 확실한 계획이 없을 때 종종 사용됩니다. 그러므로 예측을 할 때 "probably", "likely", "maybe"와 함께 사용됩니다.

Ex.

This week will **probably** be rainy and thundery.
Friday will **likely** be the best day for playing soccer.
* **Maybe** it will thundershower at 12 a.m.

*"Maybe" can go in front.

NOTE 2: We use "will" when making decisions right now. (지금 당장 결정할 때 "will"을 사용합니다.)

A: It's really hot in here. B: I will open a window.
A: I'm really hungry. I skipped lunch. B: I'll make you some ramyun quickly.

Exercise 6 *Use the information to make answers.*

Ex. Susan has a test tomorrow. She didn't study. She likely won't (likely/not) do well on the test.

1. It looks cloudy outside. It ______________ (probably) rain.
   Maybe I ______________ bring an umbrella.
2. I have a bad flu. I feel terrible. I ______________ (likely) be at school tomorrow.
3. They are having a big fight. They won't talk to each other.
   They ______________ (probably) break up.
4. We ate too much at the buffet at lunch. ______________ (maybe/not) we ______________ need dinner later.
5. He didn't sleep last night. He has class today. He ______________ (likely) stay awake in class.
6. I have an allergy to seafood. If I eat this shrimp, I ______________ (likely) get sick.

Dialogue B: *How will you study English over the vacation?*

Sofia: Hey, Akari. How will you study English over the vacation?

Akari: I'll probably 1. take some TOEIC classes. How about you, Sofia?

Sofia: I'm going to go to the U.S. to study English over the vacation.

Akari: Really? That's great! 2. Where will you visit in the U.S.?

Sofia: Well, 3. my plans are not made yet but I'll probably rent a car and drive around Hollywood. I want to see all the famous celebrities. Second, I'll go to New York and see the Statue of Liberty. Third, I'll go to Washington D.C. and see the White House. Finally, I will go to Las Vegas!

Akari: Why are you going to go to Las Vegas?

Sofia: I'll try to win a plane ticket back by playing poker!

Akari: That last part 4. seems like a bad idea.

Sofia: I'm joking. I will see some great shows in Las Vegas. I probably won't gamble at all.

Akari: Probably?

Sofia: 5. Lighten up, Akari. Classes are over. Have some fun. Maybe you should come with me. We will have a lot of fun.

Akari: I wish I had the money. I'll stay here and enjoy the beautiful weather. Promise me that you will take some pictures and send them to me!

Sofia: Of course!

Substitution Drill: Use the following responses in the above conversation. Practice each with a partner two times. Try to pronounce each word correctly.

		A	B
1.	take some TOEIC classes.	sign up for some TOEIC classes.	study some TOEIC over the vacation.
2.	Where will you visit in the U.S.?	Where are you going in the U.S.A.?	What do you want to see and do in America?
3.	my plans are not made yet	nothing is confirmed yet	I haven't made any real plans yet
4.	seems like a bad idea.	could be trouble.	might not be a good thing to do.
5.	Lighten up,	Don't be so serious,	Chill out,

Conversation Corner: *REASON FOR BEING LATE!*

- First, you should be aware that "late" is a cultural concept. In Korea and many cultures, being a few minutes late can be ok. However, certain cultures (especially Canada, U.S.A., and Japan), being late is very unacceptable. It is considered rude to the person waiting.
  우선 "늦는다"는 것은 문화적인 개념임을 알아야 합니다. 한국과 많은 문화권에서 몇 분 늦는 것은 아무 일도 아닐 수 있습니다. 하지만 어떤 문화권 특히 캐나다와 미국 그리고 일본에서 늦는다는 것은 매우 용인되지 않는 상황입니다. 늦는다는 것은 기다리고 있는 사람에게 매우 무례한 것으로 간주됩니다.
- In fact, if you do not arrive at a job interview at least 30 minutes before the set time, you may not even get the interview, and almost certainly not the job. In the university classroom, the professor should be the last to enter.
  사실 구직 면접을 볼 때 정해진 시간보다 최소한 30분 일찍 도착하지 않으면 면접조차 볼 수 없을 수 있으며 직장을 구하기는 거의 불가능합니다. 대학 강의실에서도 교수님은 가장 늦게 들어오는 분이어야 합니다. (학생들이 시간 내에 강의실에 입장하여 앉아 있어야 한다는 의미입니다.)

As a class with the teacher, write down the reason you have been late for class, for work, and for meeting friends.

For class	For work	To meet friends
•	•	•
•	•	•
•	•	•
•	•	•
•	•	•
•	•	•

Now look above and cross out any answers that you SHOULD NOT say.

위 표현을 보고 여러분이 말하면 안되는 답은 모두 "X" 표를 하세요.

Ex: I was late because I drank too much alcohol last night. ✘

With the GOOD reasons, and using the "Apology" section, make better excuses.

Ex: Late for class: Professor, I am very sorry for being late. I missed the shuttle bus.
교수님 늦어서 죄송합니다. 통학버스를 놓쳤습니다.

- Late for class:
- Late for work:
- Late for meeting friends:
- Late for a first date:
- Late for a job interview:

Grammar Focus 2: *Questions with "Will"*

Pronoun	Affirmative	Negative(Not)	Question	
I	will go.	won't go. (will not go.)	Will I go?	Yes, I will. No, I won't. (No, I will not.)
You We They	will eat.	won't eat. (will not eat.)	Will you eat?	Yes, you will. No, you won't. (No, you will not)
	will play.	won't play. (will not play.)	Will we play?	Yes, we will. No, we won't. (No, we will not.)
	will sleep.	won't sleep. (will not sleep.)	Will they sleep?	Yes, they will. No, they won't. (No, they will not.)
He She It	will study.	won't study. (will not study.)	Will he study?	Yes, he will. No, he won't. (No, he will not.)
	will read.	won't read. (will not read.)	Will she study?	Yes, she will. No, she won't. (No, she will not.)
	will work.	won't work. (will not work.)	Will it go to work?	Yes, it will. No, it won't. (No, it will not.)

RULE: "Will" acts similar to "to be" in how it makes questions and answers.
To make a question with "Will", put "Will" before the subject (I / you / we / they / he / she / it).

He will dance tomorrow. → Will **he** dance tomorrow?

small letter

They will dance tomorrow. → Will **they** dance tomorrow?

Exercise 7 *Make sentences with the following stems and write the answers.*

1. (we/watch T.V. tomorrow) (yes)
   Will we watch T.V. tomorrow? Yes, we will.
2. (I/go fishing next vacation) (yes)
3. (she/visit her grandmother next Christmas) (no)

4. (they/use the Internet this evening) (no)

____

5. (you go swimming next week) (yes)

____

6. (John/wait for the next bus) (no)

____

7. (Lucy and Jill/go out tonight) (no)

____

8. (I/stay at home this Friday) (no)

____

9. (he/drive his car to Daejeon next weekend) (yes)

____

10. (they/have a party next Tuesday) (yes)

____

WWWWWH and Will: Just like in all other cases of question making, once you have a yes / no question, you can easily make a WHO WHAT WHERE WHEN WHY HOW question!

He will dance tomorrow. ➡ Will he dance tomorrow? ➡ **When** will (he) dance tomorrow?

small letter

They will dance tomorrow. ➡ Will they dance tomorrow? ➡ **Why** will (they) dance tomorrow?

Exercise 8 *Make WWWWWH questions:*

1. What/you do tomorrow? What will you do tomorrow?
2. When/you go on vacation? ______________________________
3. How/we get to school tomorrow? ______________________________
4. Where/they play soccer? ______________________________
5. Who/he travel to Jeju with? ______________________________
6. Why/she be late for class next week? ______________________________

TOEIC VOCABULARY

Read the following common TOEIC words. Memorize so that you can do well on the TOEIC. Write the Korean and English below in the blanks two times to help you learn.

remain: ~으로 남다.
She still remained single even in her late fifties.
(그녀는 50대 후반에도 여전히 독신이었다.)

_________ /_________ _________ /_________

free: 한가한.
What do you do in your free time?
(한가할 때 무엇을 하십니까?)

_________ /_________ _________ /_________

age: 연령.
You look young for your age.
(너는 나이에 비해 어려 보인다.)

_________ /_________ _________ /_________

bite: 한입 분량.
How about a quick bite?
(간단히 뭐 좀 먹을까?)

_________ /_________ _________ /_________

newspaper: 신문.
How often do you read a newspaper?
(얼마나 자주 신문을 보십니까?)

_________ /_________ _________ /_________

want: 원하다.
That's what I really wanted.
(그게 진정 내가 원했던 것입니다.)

_________ /_________ _________ /_________

watch: 보다.
How about watching a movie tonight?
(오늘밤 영화 볼까?)

_________ /_________ _________ /_________

come: 오다.
Why don't you come with me?
(나와 같이 가겠니?)

_________ /_________ _________ /_________

read: 읽다.
Read as many books as possible when young.
(젊을 때 가능한 한 많은 책을 읽으시오.)

_________ /_________ _________ /_________

otherwise: 그렇지 않으면.
Save a lot of money when young; otherwise,
you will want in old age.
(젊을 때 많은 돈을 저축해 놓아라;
그렇지 않으면 늙어서 어려워질 거야.)

_________ /_________ _________ /_________

while: ~하는 동안.
She fell asleep while she was reading.
(그녀는 책을 읽다가 잠들어 버렸다.)

_________ /_________ _________ /_________

unless: ~하지 않으면.
Unless you study hard now, you will regret later.
(지금 열심히 공부하지 않으면 나중에 후회하게 된다.)

_________ /_________ _________ /_________

nevertheless: 그럼에도 불구하고.
It was very cold; nevertheless, he enjoyed skiing.
(매우 추웠음에도 불구하고 그는 스키를 즐겼다.)

_________ /_________ _________ /_________

bed: 침대.
It's time you went to bed.
(자야 할 시간이다.)

_________ /_________ _________ /_________

leave: 떠나다.
She leaves Britain next week for ever.
(그녀는 다음 주에 영원히 영국을 떠난다.)

_________ /_________ _________ /_________

drive: 운전하다.
They drive to work every morning.
(그들은 매일 아침 운전하여 출근한다.)

_________ /_________ _________ /_________

march: 행진하다.
The demonstrators marched toward the station hand in hand.
(시위대는 손을 맞잡고 역을 향해 행진했다.)

__________ /__________ __________ /__________

parents: 부모.
Parents come back tomorrow night with many gifts.
(부모님은 내일 많은 선물을 가지고 돌아오신다.)

__________ /__________ __________ /__________

enter: 들어가다.
Entering the room, he tried to hide the diamond.
(방에 들어가자마자 그는 다이아몬드를 숨기려 했다.)

__________ /__________ __________ /__________

join: 합류하다.
When did you join the company?
(회사에 언제 입사하였습니까?)

__________ /__________ __________ /__________

absence: 결석, 결근.
During your absence, something important happened.
(당신이 없는 사이에 중요한 일이 일어났다.)

__________ /__________ __________ /__________

do: 하다.
What do you want me to do?
(내가 무엇을 하기를 바라세요?)

__________ /__________ __________ /__________

fulfil: 충족시키다, 완수하다.
You should fulfil your duty by all means.
(어떻게 해서라도 의무를 완수해야 한다.)

__________ /__________ __________ /__________

act: 행동하다.
You should act your age.
(나이에 맞게 행동해야지.)

__________ /__________ __________ /__________

open: 열리다, 열려있는.
This window will not open.
(이 창문이 열리지 않는구나.)

__________ /__________ __________ /__________

busy: 바쁜.
Though busy, they looked after my child.
(그들은 바빴어도 내 아이를 돌봐주었다.)

__________ /__________ __________ /__________

meet: 만나다.
She is going to meet his father in person.
(그녀는 그의 아버지를 직접 만나볼 예정이다.)

__________ /__________ __________ /__________

leave: 떠나다, 남기다.
They left the classroom after class.
(그들은 강의가 끝나자 교실을 떠났다.)

__________ /__________ __________ /__________

finish: 마치다.
When can you finish your homework?
(언제 과제를 마칠 수 있니?)

__________ /__________ __________ /__________

wonder: 궁금해 하다.
I wonder when he will come back.
(그가 언제 돌아올지 궁금해.)

__________ /__________ __________ /__________

UNIT 6-10 REVIEW

Warm-up Questions:

1. What are you good at?	I am good at ______.
2. What can't you do?	I can't ______.
3. What is something you must do every day?	I must ______.
4. What is your favorite month of the year?	My favorite month of the year is ______.
5. What is your favorite food?	My favorite food is ______.
6. What is your favorite drink?	My favorite drink is ______.
7. What kinds of movies do you like to watch?	I like to watch ______.
8. What is your favorite sport?	My favorite sport is ______.
9. Where have you travelled?	I have travelled to ______.
10. What is something you have to do every day?	I have to ______.
11. What is the most beautiful place you know?	______ is the most beautiful place I know.
12. What is your favorite subject that you study?	My favorite subject is ______.
13. When is your birthday?	My birthday is ______.
14. What is something that we all should do every day?	We all should ______
15. What is something that we all shouldn't do?	We all shouldn't ______.

Conversation Corner:

Exercise 1 *ORDER the sentences with ORDINAL NUMBERS (1st, 2nd, 3rd, 4th, 5th…). The first two are done for you. Blue is Akari. Pink is Jenny.*

문장의 순서를 서수로 정해 보세요. 첫 두 문제는 예시입니다. 파란색은 아카리이고 핑크색은 제니입니다.

_______ How has everything been with you Akari? How was your vacation?

_______ I had a really great time. I travelled around Europe with some friends. You must go there.

__1st__ Hi Akari- Long time no see. Great to see you again. Do you have some time to catch up?

__2nd__ Oh, hey Jenny. Sure. I am just saying goodbye to my friends here. (Waves goodbye to friends)

_______ That sounds fantastic. I definitely should. Which countries did you visit there?

_______ Great to catch up with you Jenny.

_______ The United Kingdom, too! I guess you have seen some really cool places. What was your favorite place?

_______ The movie club sounds like a great idea Jenny. I'm sure it will be a lot of fun.

_______ OK, I don't want you to be late. It was great to see you too Akari. See you soon.

_______ If the movie club isn't fun, I'll let you know. Listen, I've got to get going. I am running late for my part-time job.

_______ I visited France, Spain, Italy and even the United Kingdom.

_______ I am really enjoying the new semester. My professors are great and I have joined a movie club.

_______ Yes, my favorite place was the Eiffel Tower in Paris. It was really beautiful. I bought you a souvenir too. How is the new semester going for you Jenny?

Exercise 2 *Respond to the following questions FOR YOU. You can look back in the book to each chapter if necessary.*

1. How many people are there in your family?

   There are __________ people in my family.

2. What is your favorite day of the week?

   My favorite day of the week is __________ .

3. What is your favorite holiday?

   My favorite holiday is __________ because __________ .

4. What is something you must do today?

   I must __________ __________ today.

5. What is something you like doing every weekend?

   I like __________ every weekend.

6. What is your favorite kind of movie?

   My favorite kind of movie is __________ movies.

7. What is your best friend doing right now?

   __________ is __________ __________ right now. (or)

   My __________ __________ is __________ right now.

Grammar Focus: Review

Exercise 1 *Complete the following sentences using the correct form of the verb and tense.*

1. Complete the following sentences with Present Simple Tense with the correct form of "does / doesn't": .

a) My sister __________ *(not/play)* tennis every day

b) I __________ *(study)* English at school from Monday to Friday.

c) Chimpanzees __________ *(not/speak)* any language.

d) She always __________ *(wear)* skirts.

e) __________ they __________ *(travel)* by bus?

POSITIVE
I / You – do
He / She / It – does
They / We / You – do

NEGATIVE
I / You – don't
He / She / It – doesn't
We / You / They – don't

f) ______ your mom ______ *(cook)* dinner at night?

g) Jim and Joe ______ *(not/go)* to the theater on Sundays.

h) I never ______ *(comb)* my hair in the morning.

2. Complete the following sentences in the Present Continuous Tense- (Hint, "be verb" verb +ing)

a) What ______ you ______ *(eat)*?

b) Kat ______ *(open)* the window because she's hot.

c) My dog ______ *(not/sleep)* now.

d) The girls ______ *(listen)* to music now.

e) My brothers ______ *(not/watch)* T.V. now.

f) ______ she ______ *(comb)* her hair?

g) ______ Mary ______ *(copy)* from the blackboard?

3. Complete the following sentences with Present Simple or Present Continuous Tense:

a) I ______ *(not/study)* French now.

b) We always ______ *(play)* cards during break time.

c) Where ______ your grandmother ______ *(live)*?

d) Peter ______ *(not/take)* the children to school in the morning.

e) What ______ your brother ______ *(do)* every morning?

f) You ______ *(talk)* a lot!

g) What ______ John ______ *(write)* now?

h) What's that noise? Peter ______ *(play)* the guitar.

i) We ______ *(usually/travel)* to England in summer.

j) This kind of animal ______ *(eat)* meat.

k) Look! She ______ *(speak)* to a stranger.

l) I'm looking at that girl. She ______ *(wear)* a beautiful skirt.

Exercise 2 *Make YES / NO Questions from the sentences below.*

1. They are walking home. Are they walking home?
2. You are meeting friends. ______
3. George and Sally are dating. ______
4. I am studying right now. ______
5. She is playing computer games. ______
6. Sarah is watching T.V. ______
7. The birds are eating the seeds. ______
8. I am studying right now. ______

Exercise 3 *In the following exercise, use the answer to make the question.*

Replace the underlined word(s) with a "WWWWW and H" question word. The first one is done for you.

1. They are going to the movie theater. Where are they going?
2. It is wearing a small coat. ______ is it wearing?
3. I am studying in the classroom right now. ______ are you studying?
4. My best friend is going to visit Europe. ______ is going to visit Europe?

Now make answers for the questions with the answers in the parentheses ( ).

5. Why are you sleeping? (because I am tired) I am sleeping because I am tired.
6. What are they buying? (new jeans) ______
7. Who is coming to the party? (all our friends) ______
8. Where is everyone going tonight? (to the party) ______
9. When am I playing basketball? (tonight at 7 p.m.) ______

Exercise 4 *Fill in the blanks with the correct form of the verbs below.*

Fill in the blanks with the correct form of the verb "to walk".			*Fill in the blanks with the correct form of the verb "to go".*		
1. I	walk	to university every day.	6. I	go	to university every day.
2. You	______	to work every day.	7. You	______	to work every day.
3. He	______	to the park every day.	8. He	______	to the park every day.
4. They	______	to school every day.	9. They	______	to school every day.
5. She	______	home every day.	10. She	______	home every day.

Exercise 5 *Put it all together. Write full sentences for the following:*

1. (we/often watch movies)

____

2. (I/hate mushrooms)

____

3. (she/visit her grandparents every Christmas)

____

4. (they/use the Internet every evening)

____

5. (you/often go swimming)

____

6. (Peter/hate waiting for the train)

____

7. (Alice and Jane/want to go out tomorrow)

____

8. (I/usually stay home on weekends)

____

Exercise 6 *Make negative sentences with the following sentences using "DOESN'T":*

NOTE ONLY 1 "S" He doesn't plays. ✘ He doesn't play. ✔

HE SHE IT	DOESN'T

1. She ______________ *(not listen)* to music every day.
2. He ______________ *(not talk)* quietly in class.
3. It ______________ *(not eat)* dinner in the evening.
4. George ______________ *(not like)* playing soccer.
5. He ______________ *(not meet)* his friends today.
6. My neighbor ______________ *(not work)* at the bank.
7. He ______________ *(not eat)* fish tomorrow.
8. The student ______________ *(not study)* for his exam.
9. It ______________ *(not live)* in the forest.
10. The store usually ______________ *(not open)* before 1 a.m.

Exercise 7 *Practice these questions with your partner. Write your partner's responses.*

Use different ways to talk about frequency- always, 3 times a week, once a month, never, etc.

Questions	I	Partner
How often do you go to the cinema?		
How often do you eat popcorn?		
How often do you watch T.V.?		
How often do you eat vegetables?		
How often do you watch Sci-Fi's?		
How often do you watch action movies?		

How often do you watch romantic movies?		
How often do you play computer?		
How often do you write stories?		
How often do you read books?		
How often do you go to the beach?		

Exercise 8 *Look at the pictures then answer the questions.*

We use the simple present for 2 reasons.
Remember:

1. To talk about things that are generally true. (일반적으로 사실인 경우에 관해 말할 때.)
   - *I speak Korean.*
   - *He speaks Korean.*
2. To talk about habits and routines. (습관과 일상적인 상황에 관해 말할 때.)
   - *I get up at 7 a.m. every day.*
   - *She gets up at 7 a.m. every day.*

Remember ➡ if there is NO WWWWWH (who, what, where, why, when, how), then the answer is usually YES or NO!

	Does he play the violin after university? Yes, he does.
	Does Michelle study English on Fridays? No, ______________ . She ______________ shopping on Fridays.

	Does Marco play baseball at 10 a.m. on Saturdays? Yes, ____________________ .
	Do they eat lunch at 3 p.m.? No, ____________ . They ____________ lunch at 1 p.m.
	Do we walk to work? Yes, ____________________ .
	Does it sleep on the chair in the living room? No, ____________ . It ____________ on the floor.

Exercise 9 *Complete each sentence using the verbs provided in parentheses.*

* will not = won't
** "I / you / we / they / he / she / it" are all the same ➡ WILL / WON'T
조동사는 인칭과 수에 따라 변화하지 않습니다.

1. He ____________ a meeting tomorrow. (have)
2. We ____________ to Sydney. (not/go)
3. Brad ____________ in a new movie. (be)
4. I ____________ video games tonight. (not/play)
5. She ____________ him. (not/meet)
6. Sue ____________ this weekend. (not/go dancing)

7. I ______________ late for class.
(not/be)

8. It ______________ fish for lunch.
(eat)

9. You ______________ hard for final tests.
(study)

10. He ______________ the game.
(not/win)

11. They ______________ home on Sunday.
(not/stay)

12. I ______________ Chinese well.
(not/speak)

New Content: Have to / don't have to / must / should /shouldn't

Grammar Focus: *Overview*

- We use "have to" / "must" / "should + infinitive" to talk about obligation, things that are necessary to do, or to give advice about things that are a good idea to do.
  "have to / must / should + 동사원형"은 "의무", "필요한 일" 또는 하는 것이 현명한 일에 대해 "충고"를 하고자 할 때 사용한다.

- "Must" and "have to" are both used for obligation and are very similar. They are both followed by the infinitive.
  Must와 have to는 모두 "의무"를 가리킬 때 사용되며 매우 유사한 표현이다. 뒤에는 모두 동사 원형이 온다.

  Ex. *I must go now.*
  I have to go now.

> **Speaking Tip**
> –"have to" is more common in speaking
> –"must" is more common in writing.

- "Should" / "Should not" refer to good idea / strong advice / suggestions
  Should / Should not은 "좋은 생각 / 강력한 충고 / 제안"을 가리킨다.

  Ex. *You should study for your test.*
  I think you should choose the vanilla ice cream.
  You must get up early. You shouldn't sleep later tonight.

should  should not / shouldn't  (**should not = shouldn't)

Exercise 1 *Circle the correct expression for each situation below.*

1. You (should/shouldn't) brush your teeth twice a day to have healthy teeth.
2. You (shouldn't/should) go to the party tonight. You have a test in the morning.
3. It is going to rain. You (should/shouldn't) take an umbrella.

4. I really (shouldn't/should) have spent all my money on new clothes

5. They are running late. The plane (should/shouldn't) have landed by now.

Grammar Focus:

Obligation= need to do something. Must do something.

"의무"를 가리키는 need to와 must는 유사한 의미이다.

RED = STRONG
ORANGE = WEAK
GREEN = NONE

Present	Positive	Negative
have to / don't have to	strong obligation (possibly from outside) Children *have to* go to school. (sometimes 'have got to')	no obligation I *don't have to* work on Sundays. You *don't have to* eat anything you don't like.
must / mustn't	strong obligation (possibly based on the speaker's opinion) I *must* study today.	negative obligation You mustn't smoke here.
should / shouldn't	mild obligation or advice You *should* save some money.	mild negative obligation or advice You *shouldn't* smoke so much.

Exercise 2 *Circle and write the correct expressions for each set of rules from a school.*

1. Students ________ come to class on time.

   A) must B) must not C) don't have to D) can

2. Students ________ speak when the teacher is speaking.

   A) have to B) must not C) don't have to D) can

3. Students ________ wear uniforms.

   A) must B) must not C) don't have to D) can

4. Students ________ have their planners with them.

   A) have to B) must not C) don't have to D) can

5. Students ________ be at school before 7:45 a.m.

A) must B) must not C) don't have to D) can

6. Students ________ have piercings.

A) have to B) must not C) don't have to D) can

7. Students ________ clean their classrooms and restrooms.

A) must B) must not C) don't have to D) can

Exercise 3 *Talking Corner. Speaking in Pairs:*

Talking with your partner; use the expressions below to give advice on how to fix the problems. Give 1 piece of advice each. Use a mix of "should / shouldn't / must / mustn't."

상대방과 대화하기: 문제를 풀기 위한 방법에 관해 충고를 하는 아래 표현을 사용하세요. 각각 한 개씩의 충고를 해 보세요. "should / shouldn't / must / mustn't."를 골고루 사용하세요.

1. I feel tired a lot these days.

You ________________________________

2. I have a test tomorrow.

You ________________________________

3. I found money on the street.

You ________________________________

4. I got a bad mark in my English test.

You ________________________________

5. I'm thirsty.

You ________________________________

6. I don't have enough money to buy a new bicycle that I want.

You ________________________________

7. I gained 5kg last month and I want to lose weight.

You ________________________________

8. I have a job interview tomorrow but I have nothing nice to wear.

You ________________________________